zpachostew
oatbiscuits
sserolepork
xminestrone
labaisserice
ommé hotpot

the soup book

Published by Fog City Press
814 Montgomery Street
San Francisco, CA 94133 USA

Copyright © 2002 Weldon Owen Pty Ltd
Reprinted 2002 (three times)

Chief Executive Officer: John Owen
President: Terry Newell
Publisher: Lynn Humphries
Managing Editor: Janine Flew
Art Director: Kylie Mulquin
Editorial Coordinator: Tracey Gibson
Editorial Assistant: Marney Richardson
Production Manager: Martha Malic-Chavez
Business Manager: Emily Jahn
Vice President International Sales: Stuart
Laurence

Project Editors: Janine Flew and Anna Scobie
Project Designer: Jacqueline Richards
Food Photography: Valerie Martin
Food Stylist: Sally Parker
Home Economist: Valli Little

Library of Congress Cataloging-in-Publication
Data

The soup book.
        p. cm.
     Includes index.
     ISBN 1-876778-79-2
     1. Soups I. Fog City Press.

   TX757 S6342 2002
   641.8'13--dc21   2001054347

Color reproduction by Sang Choy
International Pte Ltd

Manufactured by Kyodo Printing Co.
(S'pore) Pte Ltd

Printed in Singapore

A Weldon Owen Production

the
soup
book

FOG CITY PRESS

contents

satisfying soups and stews

A few vegetables, some meat if desired, and water or stock: Soups and stews are both as simple as that, and as complex as you choose to make them. Their variety and deliciousness are limited only by your imagination and the ingredients to hand, making them some of the most useful and versatile dishes in the cook's repertoire.

Soups and stews have come a long way from their origins as humble staples, made from whatever meager ingredients were available. Now they run the culinary gamut from quick snack to family meal to gourmet indulgence. Their simplicity lends itself to endless interpretations: a hearty and nutritionally balanced one-bowl meal, a chilled soup for a summer's day, a delicate consommé to stimulate the palate, or a rich and creamy soup fit for an elegant dinner party.

These dishes are a boon to the busy cook, too, because although many soups and stews require a long cooking time, they take little time to prepare. A bit of chopping, perhaps some sautéing, then it's time to sit back and relax while they cook, filling the house with delicious aromas to whet the appetite for the meal ahead. Better still, most can be prepared ahead and then reheated with no deterioration in taste or texture; on the contrary, many soups and stews improve in flavor when allowed to mature for a day or two before being served. Another advantage of soups and stews is that they are economical. They can be made with cheaper cuts of meat that benefit from long, slow simmering, becoming meltingly tender and imbued with the flavors of the vegetables and herbs with which they are cooked.

This book presents over 150 recipes from around the world, from classic dishes such as Wonton Soup and Chili con Carne to contemporary recipes such as microwave Gingered Carrot Soup. Try Lobster Stew from Spain, Saffron Mussel Stew from Mexico, Greek Meatball Soup with Egg and Lemon, Italian Mixed Vegetable Soup, or Cantonese Noodle Soup. Also included are recipes for accompaniments such as muffins and quickbreads that will transform a bowl of soup or stew into a complete meal. There are also useful tips throughout the text, from hints on selecting and storing ingredients to ideas for tasty, colorful garnishes. And no book about soups would be complete without recipes for meat, chicken, fish, and vegetable stocks, the flavorsome basis for all good soups and stews. Whatever the occasion or season, with *The Soup Book* in your kitchen, you'll never be short of delicious mealtime inspiration.

soups *with* vegetables

vegetable stock

makes 5 cups (40 fl oz/1.25 l)

2 tablespoons extra virgin olive oil

1 cup (5 oz/155 g) diced carrot

¾ cup (4 oz/125 g) diced celery

¾ cup (2 oz/60 g) sliced leeks

1 small clove garlic

1 small red (Spanish) onion, cut in half

12 oz (375 g) fresh white mushrooms, cut in halves

8 cups (2 qt/2 l) cold water

1 small plum (Roma) tomato

½ teaspoon fresh thyme leaves or ¼ teaspoon dried thyme

½ teaspoon fresh marjoram leaves or ¼ teaspoon dried marjoram

4 fresh parsley sprigs

salt and ground black pepper

❖ Heat the oil in a saucepan over low heat. Add the carrot, celery, and leeks and cook, stirring often, for 3–4 minutes, until softened.

❖ Add the garlic, onion, and mushrooms and stir for 2 minutes, until the onion softens.

❖ Add the water and bring to a boil. Using a large spoon, skim any scum from the surface. Add the tomato, thyme, marjoram, and parsley. Reduce heat and simmer, uncovered, for 1 hour.

❖ Strain the stock through a fine-mesh sieve lined with cheesecloth (muslin) into an airtight container. Season with salt and pepper. Use immediately, or cool, cover, and refrigerate for up to 3 days or freeze for up to 1 month.

roasted vegetable stock

makes 4 cups (32 fl oz/1 liter)

8 oz (250 g) fresh button mushrooms

1 onion, cut into fourths

2 carrots, peeled, cut into chunks

8 cloves garlic, peeled, bruised

1 small turnip, peeled, cut into chunks

7 cups (56 fl oz/1.75 l) water

1 bouquet garni (sprigs of fresh herbs, such as parsley, thyme, oregano, and marjoram, plus a bay leaf and pinch of crushed dried chile flakes, wrapped in cheesecloth/muslin)

salt

❖ Preheat an oven to 400°F (200°C/Gas Mark 5). Lightly grease a roasting pan, add the mushrooms, onion, carrots, garlic, and turnip and toss well. Roast, tossing occasionally, until well browned, about 1 hour.

❖ Transfer the vegetables to a stockpot. Add 1 cup (8 fl oz/250 ml) of the water to the hot roasting pan and stir to dislodge any cooked bits on the base of the pan. Add to the stockpot with the rest of the water and the bouquet garni. Simmer gently, uncovered, until the vegetables are soft, 45–60 minutes.

❖ Strain the liquid through a fine-mesh sieve into an airtight container, pressing on the solids left in the sieve to extract as much liquid as possible. Season to taste with salt. Allow to cool, then refrigerate until required.

vegetable
soup base

makes about 32 cups
(8 qt/8 l)

This recipe converts an abundance of summer produce from your garden or the market into the ideal base for a quick, tasty soup. You will need four 8-cup (2 qt/2-l) sterilized jars and a pressure canner. To sterilize jars, fill with boiling water and set aside for 10 minutes. Pour out the water, turn the jars upside down, and dry on kitchen towels.

6 cups (48 fl oz/1.5 l) water

12 large, ripe tomatoes, peeled and chopped

6 medium potatoes, peeled and chopped

1 lb (500 g) fresh lima beans

kernels from 9 ears of corn

12 medium carrots, peeled and thickly sliced

4 celery stalks, sliced

2 medium onions, chopped

2 teaspoons salt

vegetable soup base

❖ Combine all the ingredients, except for the salt, in a large stockpot and bring to a boil. Boil for 5 minutes. Ladle the vegetable mixture into four 8-cup (64 fl oz/ 2-l) clean, hot, sterilized jars, ensuring that 1 inch (2.5 cm) headspace is left.

❖ Add ½ teaspoon salt to each jar. Gently tap the jars on a bench to release any air bubbles. Clean the rims of the jars and seal.

❖ Place the jars in a pressure canner and process at 10 lb (5 kg) pressure for 1¼ hours.

❖ Allow the pressure gauge to return to zero, then remove the jars from the canner and cool.

recipe hint

Cut the vegetables to roughly the same size, so they will cook in the same amount of time. Pre-cooking the vegetables allows them to be packed more tightly, therefore requiring fewer jars. Label the jars and store in a dark, cool, dry place.

leek and pumpkin soup

2 teaspoons butter

3 lb (1.5 kg) pumpkin, peeled and cubed

6 leeks, trimmed and sliced

8 cups (64 fl oz/2 l) milk

salt

Melt the butter in a large saucepan, add the pumpkin and leeks, and cook until browned. Stir in two-thirds of the milk and season to taste with salt. Cook over very low heat for about 3 hours, or until the milk is absorbed. Transfer to a blender, add the remaining milk, and blend until smooth. (Work in batches if necessary.) Return the soup to the pan and heat over low heat until warmed through. Serve immediately in warmed bowls.

neapolitan
herb soup

serves 6

3 eggs

pinch of salt

2 ripe medium tomatoes

3 tablespoons
extra virgin olive oil

6 medium zucchini
(courgettes), diced

8 cups (64 fl oz/2 l) chicken
stock, boiling

1 tablespoon chopped
fresh basil

1 tablespoon chopped
fresh parsley

ground black pepper

❖ Place the eggs and salt in a bowl and lightly beat.

❖ Immerse the tomatoes in boiling water for 1 minute, then peel and dice.

❖ Heat the oil in a saucepan over medium heat. Add the zucchini and cook, stirring, for 2 minutes. Add the hot stock and bring to a boil. Boil for 2 minutes.

❖ Remove from the heat, and add the egg mixture, basil, parsley, and pepper. Whisk constantly over very low heat for 1 minute, until thickened. Stir in the tomatoes, season to taste with pepper, and serve.

creamy
fresh pea soup

serves 4

2 tablespoons butter

1 onion, chopped

1 lettuce heart (2 oz/60 g),
finely shredded

4 cups (32 fl oz/1 liter)
chicken stock

2 lb (1 kg) fresh peas, shelled,
or fava (broad) beans, shelled

salt and ground black pepper

⅓ cup (2½ fl oz/80 ml) crème
fraîche or sour cream

4 sprigs fresh chervil

❖ Melt the butter in a large saucepan. Add the onion
and stir over low heat for 2 minutes, until softened.
Add the lettuce and stir for 2 minutes more.

❖ Stir in the chicken stock and bring to a boil.

❖ Stir in the peas or beans and cook for 20 minutes,
or until tender. Season to taste with salt and pepper.

❖ Reserve ¼ cup of the cooked peas or beans. Place
the remaining peas or beans and the liquid in a blender
and blend until smooth. Strain through a fine-mesh
sieve into the pan, then bring to a boil. Add the crème
fraîche or sour cream, stir well, and remove from heat.

❖ Serve immediately, garnished with the reserved
peas or beans and the chervil.

provençal garlic soup

serves 4–6

Despite the prodigious
amount of garlic in this
recipe, the resulting soup
is surprisingly mellow.
Trim any green tips from
the garlic cloves, as they
carry the sharp flavor.

8 cups (2 qt/2 l) water

¾ cup (3 oz/90 g) garlic cloves, peeled

¼ cup (2 fl oz/60 ml) extra virgin olive oil

½ cup (2 oz/60 g) sliced white onion

⅓ cup (1⅓ oz/40 g) sliced celery

⅓ cup (1⅓ oz/40 g) sliced fennel

½ cup (4 fl oz/125 ml) dry white wine

4 fresh thyme sprigs

½ teaspoon fresh rosemary leaves

1 bay leaf

5 cups (40 fl oz/1.25 l) chicken stock

2¼ cups (18 fl oz/560 ml) heavy (double) cream

1 slice coarse country bread, preferably 1 day old, chopped

1 tablespoon salt

1 teaspoon ground white pepper

❖ Place the water and garlic in a large saucepan and bring to a boil over high heat. Reduce the heat to medium and simmer, uncovered, until the garlic is translucent, about 5 minutes. Drain and reserve the garlic.

❖ Return the saucepan to medium heat. Add the olive oil and heat for 30 seconds. Add the onion, celery, and fennel and cook, stirring, until just tender, 2–3 minutes. Add the garlic cloves, reduce the heat slightly, and cook, stirring often, for 2 minutes. Do not allow the garlic to brown. Stir in the wine and cook until the liquid has reduced by half.

❖ Add the thyme, rosemary, bay leaf, stock, cream, bread, salt, and pepper. Stir well, reduce the heat to low, and simmer, uncovered, stirring occasionally, until the soup has reduced by one-fourth and is cream-colored, about 40 minutes. Set aside for 10 minutes to cool slightly.

❖ Transfer half of the soup to a blender and blend until smooth. Place in a large bowl and then blend the remaining soup until smooth. Return all the soup to the pan.

❖ Reheat the soup over medium heat. Serve immediately.

corn, zucchini, and cilantro soup

serves 6

2 tablespoons vegetable oil

kernels from 3 ears of corn

1 tablespoon finely
chopped onion

6 cups (48 fl oz/1.5 l)
chicken stock

3 zucchini (courgettes),
cut into ⅓-inch (8-mm) cubes
or coarsely grated

6 tablespoons finely chopped
cilantro (fresh coriander)

salt and ground black pepper

4 oz (125 g) queso fresco,
farmer's cheese, or mild feta,
cut into ½-inch (13-mm) cubes

❖ Heat the oil in a medium saucepan over medium heat. Add the corn and cook, stirring occasionally, for 6–8 minutes, or until softened. Add the onion and cook, stirring, until it is translucent.

❖ Stir in 2 cups (16 fl oz/500 ml) of the stock and cook until the corn is tender. Add the remaining stock, zucchini, cilantro, and salt and pepper to taste. Bring to a boil, then reduce heat and simmer until the zucchini is just tender.

❖ Serve immediately, accompanied by the cheese.

cheese broth

serves 6

8 oz (250 g) potatoes, cut into ¼-inch (6-mm) cubes and rinsed

2 teaspoons salt

2 tablespoons vegetable oil

2 tablespoons finely chopped onion

9 oz (280 g) tomatoes, chopped

pinch of baking soda (bicarbonate of soda)

1 cup (8 fl oz/250 ml) hot water

3 cups (24 fl oz/750 ml) milk

8 oz (250 g) mozzarella cheese, shredded

12 dried pequin chiles, crushed, or 1 teaspoon dried chile flakes

❖ Place the potatoes in a small saucepan and add enough water to cover. Add 1 teaspoon of the salt and bring to a boil. Boil until the potatoes are cooked but still firm, about 15 minutes. Drain and set aside.

❖ Heat the oil in a medium saucepan over low heat and cook the onion, stirring often, until it softens.

❖ Place the tomatoes in a blender and blend until smooth. Strain into the saucepan. Add the remaining salt, baking soda, potatoes, and hot water. In another saucepan, bring the milk just to a boil and stir in to the tomato mixture. Simmer for 2–3 minutes, or until heated through.

❖ Place the cheese in a soup tureen. Add the soup and stir until the cheese melts. Sprinkle serving bowls with the chiles or chile flakes, then ladle in the soup.

chickpea soup

with swiss chard and tomatoes

serves 4

Chickpeas (garbanzo beans) and Swiss chard both have a delicious, earthy nuttiness that is particularly suited to creating full-flavored vegetarian soups.

2 tablespoons extra virgin olive oil

1 yellow onion, coarsely chopped

3 cloves garlic, finely chopped

8 small plum (Roma) tomatoes, coarsely chopped

1 bunch Swiss chard (silverbeet)

1 can (16 oz/500 g) chickpeas (garbanzo beans), drained

6 cups (48 fl oz/1.5 l) water

salt and ground black pepper

4 slices coarse country bread, toasted

❖ Heat the olive oil in a large saucepan over medium heat. Add the onion and cook, stirring often, until softened but not browned, 3–4 minutes. Add the garlic and stir for a few seconds. Add the tomatoes, increase the heat to medium-high, and cook, stirring occasionally, until the tomatoes begin to break down and form a sauce, about 10 minutes.

❖ Meanwhile, remove and discard the bottom third of the chard stems. Cut the remaining stem portions crosswise into ¼-inch (6-mm) wide pieces. Stack several chard leaves together, roll them up lengthwise, then cut crosswise to form ribbons ¼-inch (6-mm) wide. Repeat with the remaining chard leaves.

❖ Add the chard, chickpeas, and water to the saucepan and bring the mixture to a simmer over medium-high heat. Simmer, uncovered, until the vegetables are tender and the flavors have blended, 30–45 minutes. The soup will be chunky, with the consistency of a broth.

❖ Season to taste with salt and pepper. Place a slice of toast in each serving bowl. Ladle the soup over and serve immediately.

summer squash soup

makes 16 cups (4 qt/4 l)

½ cup (4 oz/125 g) butter

20–24 (2¼ lb/1.125 kg) small
yellow crookneck squash, sliced

1 clove garlic, finely chopped

2 large onions, chopped

10 oz (315 g) broccoli, chopped

3–4 tablespoons all-purpose
(plain) flour

2 cups (16 fl oz/500 ml)
whole or skim milk

pinch of fresh thyme leaves

2 cups (16 fl oz/500 ml)
chicken stock

❖ Melt the butter in a frying pan. Add the squash, garlic, and onions and cook, stirring, until softened. Add the broccoli and cook, stirring, until it softens.

❖ Stir in the flour, being careful not to let the mixture burn. When well combined and slightly cooked, remove from the heat and gradually stir in the milk and thyme.

❖ Return the pan to the heat and stir in the stock. Cook until thickened, then reduce the heat to low and simmer for 5 minutes.

❖ Serve immediately or freeze for up to 2 months.

ancho chile
and ricotta soup

makes 5 cups (40 fl oz/1.25 l)

2 oz (60 g) ancho chiles, toasted on
a griddle or dry-fried in a frying pan,
then stemmed and soaked in
warm water until soft

8 oz (250 g) tomatoes, charred on a
griddle, or in a dry frying pan

1 thick slice onion, lightly charred

1 clove garlic, lightly charred, then peeled

4 cups (32 fl oz/1 liter) chicken stock

2 tablespoons vegetable oil

2 tablespoons butter

7 oz (220 g) ricotta cheese

salt

2 tablespoons coarsely chopped
cilantro (fresh coriander)

❖ Place the chiles, tomatoes, onion, garlic, and 2 cups (16 fl oz/500 ml) of the stock in a blender and blend until smooth.

❖ Heat the oil and butter in a medium casserole. Strain the chile mixture into the casserole and cook, stirring occasionally, for 5 minutes. Place the remaining stock and the ricotta in a blender and blend until smooth. Add to the casserole and season to taste with salt. Cook over medium heat until hot. Serve sprinkled with cilantro.

vichyssoise

serves 4

¼ cup (2 oz/60 g) butter

3 leeks, washed and
thinly sliced

1 onion, finely chopped

salt and ground black pepper

5 cups (40 fl oz/1.25 l)
chicken stock

1 lb (500 g) all-purpose
potatoes, peeled and
thinly sliced

crème fraîche, for garnishing

4 sprigs fresh chervil,
for garnishing

❖ Heat the butter in a large saucepan. Add the leeks, onion, and salt and pepper to taste. Cover and cook over low heat until the vegetables are soft, but not browned. Add the stock and potatoes and bring to a boil. Reduce the heat and simmer until the potatoes are tender. Remove from the heat and allow to cool.

❖ Place the mixture in a food processor and process until smooth. If serving the soup hot, return to the pan and reheat gently over low heat. If serving chilled, place in an airtight container in the refrigerator for several hours. Serve garnished with the crème fraîche and chervil sprigs.

chile corn soup

serves 10

6 long fresh green chiles

¼ cup (2 fl oz/60 ml) vegetable oil

2 onions, chopped

3 cloves garlic, crushed

4 tomatoes, peeled, seeded, and chopped

10 cups (2½ qt/2.5 l) chicken stock

2 cups (10 oz/315 g) fresh corn kernels

8 oz (250 g) mild-flavored cheese, shredded

❖ Cook the chiles under a hot broiler (grill), turning occasionally, until the skin blisters and blackens. Place in a heatproof bowl, cover with plastic wrap, and set aside for 30 minutes. Peel the chiles and cut into strips.

❖ Heat the oil in a large saucepan over low heat. Add the onions and cook, stirring often, for 5 minutes, or until softened. Add the garlic and stir for 1 minute. Add the tomatoes and cook until the mixture forms a smooth paste. Stir in the stock and bring to a boil. Add the corn, reduce the heat, and simmer for 10 minutes, or until the corn is tender. Serve immediately, garnished with the shredded cheese.

wild mushroom soup

serves 4–6

In Umbria, a region in the heart of Italy, soups are often made from an extraordinary assortment of mushrooms that are gathered during family outings in the woods. In this recipe, a mixture of fresh shiitake and cremini or white mushrooms is used.

⅓ cup (2 oz/60 g) pine nuts

½ cup (4 fl oz/125 ml) extra virgin olive oil

1 large yellow onion, finely chopped

3 cloves garlic, finely chopped

10 plum (Roma) tomatoes, chopped

1 lb (500 g) fresh shiitake mushrooms, stems removed, sliced

8 oz (250 g) fresh cremini or white mushrooms, stems removed, sliced

6 cups (48 fl oz/1.5 l) water

1 tablespoon chopped fresh basil

1 tablespoon chopped fresh flat-leaf (Italian) parsley

1 tablespoon chopped fresh rosemary

1 tablespoon chopped fresh thyme

salt and ground black pepper

❖ Preheat an oven to 350°F (180°C/Gas Mark 4). Spread the pine nuts over a baking sheet and toast in the oven until golden and fragrant, about 5–8 minutes. Remove from the oven and set aside to cool.

❖ Heat the olive oil in a large saucepan over medium heat. Add the onion and cook, stirring often, until soft and golden, about 5 minutes. Add the garlic, tomatoes, and mushrooms and increase the heat to high. Cook, stirring often, until the mushrooms begin to release their liquid, about 7 minutes.

❖ Stir in the water and herbs and bring the mixture to a boil. Reduce the heat to medium-low and simmer, uncovered, stirring occasionally, until the vegetables are tender, 25–30 minutes. Season to taste with salt and pepper. Serve immediately, sprinkled with the pine nuts.

recipe variations

You can substitute any full-flavored mushrooms in this recipe, whether they are cultivated or wild, including champignons, chanterelles, morels, and porcini.

hearty
peasant soup

serves 6

1 lb (500 g) ripe tomatoes

2 tablespoons extra virgin olive oil

1 onion, chopped

1 clove garlic, chopped

8 cups (64 fl oz/2 l) beef stock

salt and ground black pepper

10 oz (315 g) ditalini (short pasta tubes)

6 slices coarse country bread

❖ Immerse the tomatoes in boiling water for 1 minute, then peel and chop. Heat the oil in a large saucepan over low heat and cook the onion and garlic, stirring often, until translucent. Stir in the tomatoes and stock, and season to taste with salt and pepper. Simmer, uncovered, for 1 hour. Stir in the pasta and cook until al dente.

❖ Toast the slices of bread. Place 3 slices in a soup tureen and pour over the boiling soup. Break the remaining slices of toast into pieces. Serve the soup immediately, garnished with the pieces of toast.

mushroom and chile soup

serves 6

1½ lb (750 g) fresh white
mushrooms, sliced

1½ teaspoons salt

1 lb (500 g) tomatoes, roasted
on a cast-iron griddle or fried in
a frying pan

1 thick slice onion, toasted on
a cast-iron griddle or fried in
a frying pan

1 clove garlic, toasted on
a cast-iron griddle or fried in
a frying pan

2 cascabel chiles; 1 toasted and
seeded, the other whole

1 tablespoon vegetable oil

1 tablespoon butter

4 cups (32 fl oz/1 liter)
chicken stock

✤ Place the mushrooms and salt in a saucepan with just enough boiling water to cover. Cook over high heat for 2–3 minutes, until the mushrooms are tender. Drain.

✤ Place the tomatoes, onion, and garlic in a blender. Add half of the mushrooms and the toasted chile and blend until smooth.

✤ Heat the oil and butter in a casserole. Strain the tomato mixture into the casserole and simmer for 4 minutes. Stir in the stock, the remaining mushrooms, and the whole chile. Taste and season with salt, if necessary. Bring the mixture to a boil, then boil for 3 minutes. Serve immediately.

vegetable soup

⅓ cup (2½ fl oz/80 ml) extra virgin olive oil

½ onion, thinly sliced

12 oz (375 g) cabbage, finely chopped

1 lettuce, finely chopped

10 oz (315 g) spinach, finely chopped

10 oz (315 g) Swiss chard (silverbeet), finely chopped

1 celery stalk, finely chopped

8 cups (64 fl oz/2 l) beef stock

salt and ground black pepper

8 oz (250 g) shelled fresh peas

6 slices coarse country bread

2 cloves garlic, cut in halves

1 tablespoon chopped fresh parsley

◈ Heat half of the oil in a large saucepan over high heat. Add the onion and cook until translucent. Reduce the heat to low and add the cabbage, lettuce, spinach, chard, and celery. Simmer, stirring from time to time, for 15 minutes. Add the stock and salt and pepper to taste, then bring to a boil. Reduce heat and simmer for 2 hours. Stir in the peas and cook for 15 minutes.

◈ Toast the bread slices. While they are still hot, rub them with the cut sides of the garlic cloves. Place the slices of toast in a soup tureen and pour the hot soup over them. Sprinkle with the parsley, drizzle with the remaining oil, and serve.

pumpkin
soup with rice

serves 6

1½ lb (750 g) pumpkin, seeded
and cut into large cubes

1 teaspoon salt

3 cups (24 fl oz/750 ml) milk

3 tablespoons butter

1 tablespoon grated onion

¼ cup (2 oz/60 g) cooked rice

ground black pepper

✥ Place the pumpkin in a large saucepan with enough hot water to cover. Add the salt and cook until the pumpkin is tender. Drain. Scrape the pumpkin flesh from the skin. Discard the skin. Working in batches, place some of the pumpkin flesh in a blender, add some of the milk, and blend until smooth. Repeat with the remaining pumpkin and milk.

✥ Melt the butter in the saucepan and cook the onion over medium heat until it is translucent. Add the pumpkin mixture and the rice.

✥ Season with plenty of pepper and cook over low heat, stirring occasionally, for 15 minutes. Serve.

✥ This soup can be prepared up to 2 hours in advance and reheated just before serving, if desired.

bread soup
with cilantro, garlic, and poached egg

serves 4

This Portuguese soup is known as a *sopa seca*, or "dry soup", because its primary ingredient is bread. Each serving is topped with a poached egg that is broken and swirled into the soup before eating.

1 tablespoon finely chopped garlic

1 teaspoon salt

1 cup (1⅓ oz/40 g) chopped cilantro (fresh coriander)

pinch of dried chile flakes (optional)

½ cup (4 fl oz/125 ml) olive oil

3 thick slices coarse country bread, crusts removed, cut into 1½-inch (4-cm) cubes

4 eggs

3–4 cups (24–32 fl oz/750 ml–1 liter) chicken stock

◈ Combine the garlic, salt, ½ cup (¾ oz/20 g) of the cilantro, and the chile flakes (if using) in a mortar. Pound with a pestle until the mixture forms a paste. Add ¼ cup (2 fl oz/60 ml) of the olive oil, 1 tablespoon at a time, and mix until well combined. Divide the garlic paste among 4 warmed soup bowls and keep warm.

◈ Meanwhile, preheat an oven to 350°F (180°C/Gas Mark 4). Brush the bread cubes with the remaining oil and toast in the oven, turning occasionally, until golden brown, 8–10 minutes.

◈ Divide the toasted bread cubes among the soup bowls and toss them in the garlic paste.

◈ Bring a generous amount of water to a boil in a deep frying pan. Reduce the heat to medium-low, so the water is barely simmering. Crack each egg and gently release it just above the surface of the water. Simmer until the whites are just set and the yolks are still runny, about 3 minutes. Using a slotted spoon, carefully transfer the eggs to a plate lined with paper towel.

◈ Bring the chicken stock to a boil and ladle into each soup bowl, using only enough to cover the toasted bread cubes. Carefully slip a poached egg into the center of each bowl. Sprinkle with the remaining cilantro and serve immediately.

tomato and bell pepper
soup
with chile cream

serves 6

2 red bell peppers (capsicums)

2 tablespoons oil

1 large onion, chopped

2 cloves garlic, chopped

3/4 cup (6 fl oz/180 ml) sherry

8 medium tomatoes, peeled and seeded

4 cups (32 fl oz/1 liter) chicken stock

1 bay leaf

3 sprigs fresh thyme

1 sprig fresh basil

1 large sprig fresh parsley

1 tablespoon black peppercorns

1 cup (8 fl oz/250 ml) heavy (double) cream

1/2 lemon, juiced

salt and ground black pepper

CHILE CREAM

1 long fresh green chile

1 clove garlic

5 spinach leaves, blanched in hot water

1/3 cup (2 1/2 fl oz/80 ml) heavy (double) cream, well chilled

1 tablespoon fresh lime juice

salt and ground black pepper

❖ Cook the bell peppers under a hot broiler (grill), turning occasionally, until the skin blisters and blackens. Place in a heatproof bowl, cover with plastic wrap, and set aside for 10 minutes. Peel and roughly chop.

❖ Heat the oil in a large saucepan. Add the onion and garlic and cook until softened. Add the sherry and cook until it evaporates. Stir in the tomatoes and stock. Tie the herbs and peppercorns in a square of cheesecloth (muslin) and add to the pan. Cook for 10 minutes, or until the mixture has reduced by a third. Stir in the cream and bell peppers. Simmer for 15 minutes, or until the liquid reduces slightly. Remove and discard the cheesecloth bag. Transfer to a food processor and process until smooth. Add the lemon juice and season to taste with salt and pepper.

❖ For the chile cream, place the chile, garlic, and spinach in a food processor and process until smooth. Add the cream and process until combined. Add the lime juice and season with salt and pepper. Serve the soup topped with a dollop of chile cream.

recipe hint

A bouquet garni is a small bunch of fresh herbs that are tied together, or secured in cheesecloth (muslin), and used to flavor stocks, soups, stews, casseroles, and sauces. The bouquet garni is always discarded before serving. A classic combination is 2 sprigs of parsley, 1 sprig of thyme, and a bay leaf, but rosemary, marjoram, sage, peppercorns, and even chile are sometimes added.

1½ lb (750 g) thin
asparagus spears

9 sprigs fresh chervil

1½ tablespoons extra
virgin olive oil

4 cups (32 fl oz/1 liter)
water

1 tablespoon arrowroot or
cornstarch (cornflour)

1 cup (8 fl oz/250 ml) milk

¼ teaspoon ground
nutmeg

salt and ground pepper

3 tablespoons crème
fraîche or sour cream

❖ Cut 1¼ inches (3 cm) from the tips of the asparagus and reserve. Thinly slice the remaining asparagus into rounds. Rinse the chervil and pat dry. Heat the oil in a heavy-based saucepan. Add the asparagus rounds and cook, stirring, for 5 minutes, or until just browned. Add the chervil and water. Bring to a boil. Reduce heat and simmer for 15 minutes.

❖ Place the asparagus mixture in a food processor and process until smooth. Strain the mixture to remove the solids. Return the strained liquid to the pan. Discard the contents of the sieve.

❖ Blend the arrowroot or cornstarch with the milk until smooth, then add to the pan. Add the nutmeg and season to taste with salt and pepper. Bring the mixture to a boil over low heat. Add the asparagus tips and cook, stirring, for 4 minutes, or until the tips are just cooked and the soup is thick. Remove from the heat, add the crème fraîche or sour cream, and stir to combine. This soup may be serve hot or chilled.

cream of
asparagus soup

minestrone
with pasta

serves 6

¼ cup (2 fl oz/60 ml) extra virgin olive oil

1 small onion, finely chopped

1 clove garlic, finely chopped

1 celery stalk, finely chopped

10 oz (315 g) shelled fresh young peas

3 tablespoons yellow cornmeal (polenta)

8 cups (2 qt/2 l) beef stock

10 oz (315 g) fresh or 5 oz (155 g) dried linguine or tagliatelle

salt and ground black pepper

1 handful fresh basil leaves

❖ Heat the oil in a frying pan over low heat. Add the onion, garlic, and celery and cook, stirring often, for 5 minutes. Add the peas, sprinkle with the cornmeal, and mix well. Stir in the stock and cook, covered, for 30 minutes over low heat.

❖ Add the pasta, salt, and pepper and cook until the pasta is al dente. Pour the soup into a tureen, sprinkle with the basil, and serve immediately.

39

summer vegetable soup with pesto

serves 8

1 tablespoon vegetable oil

2 onions, coarsely chopped

1 can (1 lb/500 g) tomatoes, chopped,
juice reserved

8 cups (2 qt/2 l) chicken stock

4 carrots, peeled and thinly sliced

2 potatoes, diced

4 leeks (white parts only), thinly sliced

2 large celery stalks with leaves,
thinly sliced

2 cups (10 oz/315 g) sliced green beans

1 medium zucchini (courgette), sliced

¾ cup (3 oz/90 g) broken-up spaghetti
(about 2½-inch/6-cm lengths)

1 cup (6 oz/185 g) dried great Northern
(white haricot) beans, soaked, cooked
until tender, and drained

PESTO

2 cloves garlic

¾ cup (¾ oz/20 g) fresh
basil leaves

½ cup (2 oz/60 g) grated
Parmesan cheese

2 tablespoons olive oil

❖ Heat the oil in a frying pan over medium heat. Add the onions and cook, stirring, until tender. Add the undrained tomatoes and cook, stirring, for 8 minutes. In a large saucepan, combine the stock, tomato mixture, carrots, potatoes, leeks, and celery. Bring to a boil, then reduce heat and simmer gently for 15 minutes. Add the green beans, zucchini, spaghetti, and great Northern beans. Simmer until all of the vegetables are tender, about 10 minutes.

❖ For the pesto, place the garlic, basil, cheese, oil, and ¼ cup (2 fl oz/60 ml) of the soup liquid in a food processor and process until smooth.

❖ Serve the soup topped with a dollop of pesto.

fresh tomato
and thyme soup

serves 6

1 tablespoon olive oil

2 cloves garlic, crushed, plus 3 whole cloves

2 onions, chopped

4 lb (2 kg) tomatoes, peeled and chopped

1 tablespoon tomato paste

2 teaspoons sugar

1 bay leaf

4 large sprigs fresh thyme, plus 6 small sprigs for garnish (optional)

½ teaspoon Tabasco sauce

salt and ground pepper

½ cup (4 fl oz/125 ml) vegetable or chicken stock

❖ Heat the oil in a saucepan over medium heat. Add the crushed garlic and the onions and cook, stirring, for 5 minutes, or until the onions are soft. Stir in the tomatoes, tomato paste, sugar, bay leaf, large thyme sprigs, whole garlic cloves, Tabasco sauce, salt and pepper to taste, and stock. Simmer, uncovered, for 20 minutes or until tomatoes are soft and the liquid has reduced by about a third.

❖ Remove and discard the bay leaf, thyme, and garlic cloves. Blend or process the soup until smooth, then return to the pan and reheat. Serve garnished with the small sprigs of thyme, if desired.

fresh tomato and thyme soup;
corn bread (page 46)

43

sicilian
vegetable soup

serves 4

*2 lb (1 kg) medium
eggplants (aubergines)*

salt

*1/3 cup (2 1/2 fl oz/80 ml)
olive oil*

*1 lb (500 g) onions,
thinly sliced*

*1 lb (500 g) ripe tomatoes,
seeded and cut into strips*

2 tablespoons capers, rinsed

2–3 celery stalks, chopped

*6 oz (185 g) black
olives, pitted*

*2 cups (16 fl oz/500 ml)
tomato juice*

*2 cups (16 fl oz/500 ml)
vegetable or chicken stock*

*1/3 cup (2 1/2 fl oz/80 ml)
vinegar (use any kind)*

1 teaspoon sugar

❖ Wash the eggplants and cut into small pieces. Place in a large colander or sieve and sprinkle with salt. Set aside for at least 1 hour to drain.

❖ Meanwhile, heat a third of the olive oil in a large frying pan. Add the onions and cook, stirring, until golden. Stir in the tomatoes, capers, celery, and olives and cook for 15 minutes. Set aside.

❖ Rinse the eggplants and dry thoroughly on paper towels. Heat the remaining oil in a frying pan over high heat. When the oil reaches its maximum temperature, add the eggplant and fry until well browned. Drain on paper towels.

❖ Stir the fried eggplant into the tomato mixture. Add the tomato juice, stock, vinegar, and sugar. Return to low heat and cook until all ingredients are heated through. Serve immediately.

corn bread

serves 6–8 as an accompaniment

1 cup (5 oz/155 g) yellow
cornmeal (polenta)

1¼ cups (5 oz/155 g)
all-purpose (plain) flour

1 teaspoon salt

1 tablespoon baking powder

1 cup (8 fl oz/250 ml) milk

2 tablespoons honey

2 eggs, well beaten

⅓ cup (3 oz/90 g) butter,
melted and cooled

½ cup (3 oz/90 g) corn kernels
(fresh or thawed frozen)

❖ Preheat an oven to 400°F (200°C/Gas Mark 5).
Butter an 8-inch (20-cm) square baking pan.

❖ Combine the cornmeal, flour, salt, and baking
powder in a large bowl. Whisk the milk, honey, and
eggs together in a jug.

❖ Using a wooden spoon, stir the egg mixture into
the cornmeal mixture until well combined. Stir in the
melted butter and then gently mix in the corn kernels.
Pour into the prepared pan.

❖ Bake until the center of the corn bread is firm to
touch, 18–20 minutes. Cut into squares and serve hot
with the soup of your choice.

pumpkin soup

serves 4–5

1 clove garlic

1 whole clove

1 sprig fresh thyme

4 cups (32 fl oz/1 liter) milk

1½ lb (750 g) pumpkin flesh,
cut into ¾-inch (2-cm) cubes

salt and ground black pepper

2 pinches grated nutmeg

2 pinches cayenne pepper

fresh sage leaves, for garnish

❖ Tie the garlic, clove, and thyme in a small square of cheesecloth (muslin).

❖ Combine the cheesecloth bag, milk, pumpkin, and a pinch of salt in a large saucepan. Bring to a boil, then reduce the heat to low. Cover and cook for 30 minutes, stirring several times during cooking.

❖ Discard the cheesecloth bag. Process the soup in a food processor until it is very smooth.

❖ Reheat the soup, stirring in the black pepper, nutmeg, and cayenne pepper. Serve immediately, garnished with sage leaves.

onion soup
gratinée

serves 6–8 as an appetizer

In the past, this hearty onion soup with melted cheese on top was served from midnight to morning in the Les Halles market district of Paris. Commonly referred to as one of the great *soupes de santé*, restorative "soups for the sick," this flavorful broth is said to work equally well on curing the flu as it does on relieving hangovers.

3 large white onions

1/2 cup (4 oz/125 g) butter

3 tablespoons all-purpose (plain) flour

8 cups (64 fl oz/2 l) beef stock, preferably homemade

salt and ground black pepper

1/2 loaf crusty French bread, preferably 1 day old

2 cups (8 oz/250 g) shredded Swiss cheese

❖ Cut the onions in half through the stem end, then thinly slice crosswise.

❖ Melt the butter in a large saucepan over medium heat. Add the onions and flour and cook, stirring often, until golden brown, about 5 minutes.

❖ Add the stock and season with salt and pepper, to taste. Bring to a boil, then reduce the heat and simmer, stirring often, until the onions are soft and translucent, about 15 minutes.

❖ Meanwhile, preheat a broiler (griller). Cut the bread diagonally into 6–8 large slices, each about ½-inch (13-mm) thick, and place them on a baking sheet. Sprinkle the bread with the cheese. Broil (grill) until the cheese melts and is golden brown, 2–3 minutes.

❖ Ladle the soup into 6–8 bowls. Place a bread slice on top of each serving of soup and serve immediately.

cream of artichoke soup

serves 6–8 as an appetizer

Only the tender hearts of artichokes are used in this smooth and mellow soup. Armagnac is a high-quality brandy that is aged in special black oak and is only produced in the Armagnac area in Gascony, France. You can substitute Cognac or any good dry brandy, if desired.

6 *medium artichokes*

1/3 *cup (2 1/2 fl oz/80 ml) olive oil*

1 *white onion, coarsely chopped*

3 *celery stalks, coarsely chopped*

1 *large russet potato, peeled and coarsely chopped*

6 *cups (48 fl oz/1.5 l) chicken stock*

1/3 *cup (2 oz/60 g) hazelnuts (filberts)*

1 *tablespoon salt*

1 *teaspoon ground white pepper*

2 *cups (16 fl oz/500 ml) heavy (double) cream*

1/3 *cup (2 1/2 fl oz/80 ml) Armagnac*

◈ Working with 1 artichoke at a time, cut off the top half. Trim the stem until it is even with the base of the artichoke. Snap or cut off the tough outer leaves until you reach the pale-green, tender leaves. Carefully open the leaves and use a small spoon to remove the prickly choke, leaving the inner leaves intact. Cut each artichoke lengthways into eighths and set aside.

◈ Preheat an oven to 400°F (200°C/Gas Mark 5).

◈ Heat the olive oil in a large saucepan over medium-high heat. Add the onion and celery and cook, stirring often, until golden brown, 8–10 minutes. Stir in the artichokes, potato, and stock and bring to a boil. Reduce the heat to medium, cover, and simmer until the mixture thickens slightly and the flavors have blended, about 45 minutes.

◈ Meanwhile, spread the hazelnuts in a single layer over a baking sheet and toast in a moderate oven for 5 minutes. Place the warm nuts on a kitchen towel, gather up the corners to form a bundle, and rub the nuts gently against each other to remove as much of the skin as possible. Cool, then chop coarsely and set aside.

◈ Working in batches, process the soup in a blender or food processor until it is smooth and creamy, about 1 minute per batch. Strain the soup through a fine-mesh sieve back into the saucepan. Stir in the salt, pepper, cream, and Armagnac, then bring to a simmer over medium heat. Serve immediately, sprinkled with the chopped hazelnuts.

kasha
vegetable casserole

serves 6

Kasha, a popular grain in Russian cookery, consists of toasted hulled buckwheat groats. Look for kasha in the cereal, grain, or flour section of your supermarket. You may substitute regular buckwheat groats, but they lack the nutty, full flavor of kasha.

1⅓ cups (10½ fl oz/330ml) chicken stock

⅔ cup (5 oz/155 g) kasha, rinsed and drained

12 cups (3 qt/3 l) water

2 tablespoons butter

1½ cups (3 oz/90 g) small broccoli florets

1 large onion, chopped

1 cup (5 oz/155 g) diced yellow crookneck squash or zucchini (courgette)

1 cup (5 oz/155 g) chopped peeled carrot

1 tablespoon finely chopped fresh basil or 1 teaspoon dried basil, crushed

½ teaspoon salt

¼ teaspoon pepper

1 cup (8 oz/250 g) ricotta cheese

1 egg, lightly beaten

1 cup (4 oz/125 g) shredded Monterey jack or mozzarella cheese

◈ In a medium saucepan combine the stock, kasha, and the water. Bring to a boil, then reduce the heat, cover and simmer until all the liquid is absorbed (allow 25 minutes for kasha and 15 minutes if using buckwheat groats).

◈ Preheat an oven to 350°F (180°C/Gas Mark 4).

◈ Meanwhile, melt the butter in a large frying pan. Add the broccoli, onion, squash or zucchini, and carrot. Cook, covered, over medium heat for 5–7 minutes, or until the vegetables are just tender. Stir in the kasha, basil, salt, and pepper. Remove from the heat.

◈ Combine the ricotta and egg in a small bowl. Spoon half of the kasha mixture into a lightly greased large casserole. Spread the ricotta mixture evenly over the top and then cover with the remaining kasha mixture. Cover and bake for 25–30 minutes, or until heated through. Uncover and sprinkle with the cheese. Bake for a further 3 minutes, or until the cheese melts. Serve at once.

poached eggs
in roasted tomato broth

This Mexican soup is sometimes called *huevos ahogados*, or "drowned eggs." To heat the tortillas in the oven, first stack them and then wrap well in aluminum foil. Place in an oven preheated to 350°F (180°C/Gas Mark 4) for 10–15 minutes, or until heated through.

4 tomatoes

4 cups (32 fl oz/1 liter) chicken stock

2 tablespoons olive oil

1 yellow onion, thinly sliced

1 teaspoon salt

$1/2$ teaspoon ground pepper

3 cloves garlic, finely chopped

2 fresh serrano chiles

8 eggs

$1/4$ cup (1 oz/30 g) grated pecorino romano or Parmesan cheese

4 large flour tortillas, heated

◈ Preheat a broiler (griller). Place the tomatoes on a shallow baking sheet in the broiler, 4–6 inches (10–15 cm) from the heat source. Broil, turning occasionally, until the tomatoes are charred all over, 10–12 minutes.

◈ Remove the tomatoes from the broiler, cool slightly, and then cut out the cores. Transfer to a blender, add 1 cup (8 fl oz/250 ml) of the stock, and blend until smooth. Set aside.

◈ Heat the olive oil in a heavy, wide saucepan over medium heat. Add the onion, salt, and pepper and cook, stirring often, until the onion is golden brown, about 15 minutes. Add the garlic and chiles and stir for 1 minute longer. Stir in the tomato mixture and remaining stock and bring to a boil. Reduce the heat to medium and simmer, uncovered, for 10 minutes to blend the flavors.

◈ Crack an egg into a small cup and gently slide it into the simmering broth. Repeat with the remaining eggs. Simmer, basting the tops of the eggs occasionally with spoonfuls of the hot broth, until the egg whites are set but the yolks are still soft, 4–6 minutes.

◈ Use a slotted spoon to gently transfer the eggs to warmed serving bowls. Ladle the broth over the eggs and sprinkle with the grated cheese. Serve immediately with the flour tortillas.

mexican garlic soup

serves 6 as an appetizer

Although garlic originally came to Mexico with the Spanish explorers, it is now so ubiquitous that this soup is a regular feature on lunch menus there. Do not be put off by the amount of garlic, as the flavor mellows and sweetens with slow cooking.

3 tablespoons olive oil

9 cloves garlic, halved

½ loaf crusty French bread, cut into 1-inch (2.5-cm) cubes

1 teaspoon salt

½ teaspoon ground black pepper

8 cups (64 fl oz/2 l) chicken stock

3 eggs, lightly beaten

2 tablespoons fresh epazote or oregano leaves, chopped

1 lime, cut into 6 wedges

✦ Preheat an oven to 325°F (160°C/Gas Mark 3). Heat the olive oil in a large saucepan over low heat. Add the garlic and cook, stirring occasionally, until the oil is well flavored and the garlic is soft but not browned, about 5 minutes. Remove from the heat and discard the garlic.

✦ Place the bread cubes in a bowl and add about half of the flavored oil (leave the remaining oil in the pan). Sprinkle with the salt and pepper and toss well to coat. Spread over a baking sheet and bake until golden brown and crisp, 10–15 minutes. Remove from oven and set aside.

✦ Add the stock to the remaining oil in the saucepan and bring to a simmer over medium heat. Gradually add the beaten eggs to the simmering stock while stirring constantly in a circular motion. Add the epazote or oregano and continue to simmer until the eggs are set, about 3 minutes more. Remove from the heat.

✦ Divide the croutons among warmed soup bowls and top with the egg-laced stock. Squeeze a wedge of lime over each bowl, then drop the wedge in the bowl. Serve immediately.

winter soup
with three vegetables

serves 4

2 tablespoons extra virgin olive oil

1 celery heart (6½ oz/200 g), cut into thin rounds

13 oz (410 g) potatoes, peeled and diced or coarsely grated

1½ lb (750 g) pumpkin flesh, diced

2 cups (16 fl oz/500 ml) water

salt and ground black pepper

❖ Heat the oil in a large saucepan. Add the celery and cook over medium-low heat for 2 minutes, stirring constantly with a wooden spoon. Add the potatoes and stir for 1 minute. Stir in the pumpkin and water. Season with salt and bring to a boil. Reduce the heat, cover, and simmer, stirring occasionally, for about 40 minutes, or until the potatoes break down.

❖ Season with pepper and serve immediately, or serve well chilled as a summer soup.

potato *casserole*

serves 4

olive oil, for deep-frying

4 large potatoes (about
1 lb 10 oz/815 g total weight),
peeled and sliced

2 eggs, beaten

all-purpose (plain) flour, for
coating, plus 2 teaspoons

4 cloves garlic, finely chopped

2 small onions (about
6½ oz/200 g total weight),
finely chopped

4 small tomatoes (about
12 oz/375 g total weight),
peeled and finely chopped

1 teaspoon sugar

1⅔ cups (13 fl oz/410 ml)
beef stock

salt

❖ Heat the olive oil in a frying pan. Dip the potato slices in the beaten egg and then toss in the flour to coat. Deep-fry the potatoes, in batches, until golden on both sides. Transfer to a heatproof casserole.

❖ Remove most of the oil from the pan. Add the garlic and onions to the pan and cook, stirring often, until they soften. Add the tomatoes and cook over low heat, stirring occasionally, until the mixture reduces a little. Stir in the sugar.

❖ Add the 2 teaspoons of flour to the tomato mixture and stir well. Pour over the potatoes. Add the stock and season with salt. Cover and cook over low heat for 30–45 minutes, until the flavors are well blended.

ratatouille-style
vegetable
stew

serves 4

1 tablespoon olive oil

1 medium onion, sliced and
separated into rings

2 cloves garlic, finely chopped

1 lb (500 g) mixed fresh vegetables,
such as sliced peeled carrots; diced peeled
parsnips, potatoes, kohlrabi, turnip, or
rutabaga (swedes); sliced celery; and/or
julienne strips of red or green bell pepper
(capsicum) or sliced zucchini (courgette)

1 medium eggplant (aubergine), cubed

1½ cups (12 fl oz/375 ml) chicken stock

2 large tomatoes, peeled (if desired)
and chopped

1 tablespoon finely chopped fresh basil
or 1 teaspoon dried basil, crushed

1 tablespoon finely chopped fresh rosemary
or 1 teaspoon dried rosemary, crushed

1 bay leaf

1 teaspoon salt

¼ teaspoon ground black pepper

❖ Heat the oil in a large saucepan. Add the onion and garlic and cook, stirring, for 5 minutes. Stir in your choice of carrots, parsnips, potatoes, kohlrabi, turnip, rutabaga, and celery, and the eggplant, stock, tomatoes, basil, rosemary, bay leaf, salt, and pepper.

❖ Bring the mixture to a boil, then reduce the heat, cover, and simmer, stirring occasionally, for 20 minutes. If using, stir in the bell pepper and zucchini. Cover and simmer for 10 minutes more. Remove the bay leaf and discard. Serve immediately.

food fact

True French ratatouille is a hearty vegetable stew of eggplant (aubergine), tomatoes, summer (baby) squash, onions, and green bell peppers (capsicums). But the choice of vegetables may be unlimited, as in this eclectic version.

chestnut and celery soup

serves 6–8 as an appetizer

During the winter months, hot roasted chestnuts are often sold by vendors on the boulevards of Paris. The meaty nut is a popular ingredient in bistros around France, either fresh or as a canned purée. This rich soup is a popular first course for Christmas luncheons and New Year celebrations.

1 lb (500 g) prepared unsweetened chestnut purée or 1½ lb (750 g) fresh chestnuts

½ cup (4 oz/125 g) butter

2 white onions, chopped

3 celery stalks, coarsely chopped

1 large russet potato, peeled and coarsely chopped

6 cups (48 fl oz/1.5 l) chicken stock

2 cups (16 fl oz/500 ml) heavy (double) cream

1 tablespoon salt

1 teaspoon ground white pepper

❖ If you are using fresh chestnuts, preheat an oven to 400°F (200°C/Gas Mark 5). Using a sharp knife, cut a cross on the flat side of each chestnut. Spread the chestnuts over a shallow baking sheet and roast until the nuts feel tender when pressed and the shells have curled where cut, 25–30 minutes. Remove from the oven and, using a small, sharp knife, remove the shells and the furry skin beneath. (The nuts are easiest to peel when still warm.) Set aside.

❖ Melt the butter in a large saucepan over medium-high heat. Add the onions and celery and cook, stirring often, until golden brown, about 5 minutes.

❖ Add the chestnut purée or roasted chestnuts. Stir in the potato, stock, and cream and bring to a boil. Add the salt and pepper, reduce the heat to medium-low, and simmer, uncovered, until the soup thickens slightly, about 1 hour.

❖ Working in batches, transfer the soup to a blender and blend until it is smooth and creamy, about 1 minute per batch.

❖ Return the soup to the pan and bring to a simmer over medium heat. Taste and adjust the seasoning, if necessary. Serve immediately.

mediterranean
vegetable casserole

serves 4

This traditional Spanish dish, also known as *tumbet*, is wonderful when freshly made, but is also delicious when served at room temperature. It can be served on its own as a main course or as an accompaniment to fish, meat, or eggs.

1 lb (500 g) eggplants (aubergines), thinly sliced

salt

2¼ cups (18 fl oz/560 ml) olive oil

1 lb (500 g) potatoes, thinly sliced

1 lb (500 g) green bell peppers (capsicums), seeded and chopped

3 cloves garlic, peeled

2 lb (1 kg) ripe tomatoes, peeled and finely chopped

◈ Place the eggplant slices in a colander, sprinkle with salt, and set aside for 1 hour to draw out the bitter juices. Rinse the eggplant well and dry with paper towels.

◈ Heat the oil in a frying pan over low heat. Add the potatoes and cook, stirring often, until they are soft but not golden. Transfer to a heatproof casserole. Add the eggplant to the frying pan and cook until soft but not golden. Arrange the eggplant on top of the potatoes. Add the bell peppers to the frying pan and cook until just soft. Use a slotted spoon to arrange the bell peppers on top of the eggplant. Sprinkle with a little salt.

◈ Drain some of the oil from the frying pan, if necessary, so there is only enough left to just cover the base of the pan. Reserve the extra oil. Add the garlic and stir over medium heat for 1 minute. Add the tomatoes and cook, stirring often, for 20–30 minutes. When the oil begins to rise to the surface, add a little salt and then strain the mixture through a fine-mesh sieve over the vegetables in the casserole.

◈ Meanwhile, preheat an oven to 350°F (180°C/Gas Mark 4). Sprinkle a little of the reserved extra oil over the top of the tomato mixture. Bake for 10 minutes. Serve hot, warm, or chilled.

tuscan vegetable soup

serves 4

1 cup (7 oz/220 g) spelt, barley,
or long-grain white rice

5 cups (40 fl oz/1.25 l) water

2 large broccoli florets

1 small leek, white part only

1 small celery stalk

1 large carrot, peeled

2 tablespoons extra virgin olive oil, plus
extra to serve

1 cup (4 oz/125 g) chopped yellow onion

1½ cups (9 oz/280 g) peeled, seeded,
and chopped plum (Roma) tomatoes
(fresh or canned)

½ cup (2½ oz/75 g) peeled and
thinly sliced white turnip

5 cups (40 fl oz/1.25 l) vegetable
or meat stock

¾ cup (3½ oz/105 g) diagonally
sliced green beans

1 small zucchini (courgette), cut in half
lengthwise, then thinly sliced crosswise

salt and ground black pepper

grated Parmesan cheese, to serve

✧ Combine the spelt, barley, or rice and 3 cups (24 fl oz/750 ml) of the water in a bowl. Set aside for 1 hour.

✧ Meanwhile, cut the broccoli, leek, celery, and carrot into ¼-inch (6-mm) thick slices.

✧ Heat the olive oil in a large saucepan over low heat. Add the onion and cook, stirring often, until it is translucent, about 5 minutes. Add the tomatoes and cook, stirring often, for 2 minutes. Drain the spelt, barley, or rice and add to the pan, along with the broccoli, leek, celery, carrot, and turnip. Cook, stirring, for 3 minutes.

✧ Stir in the stock and 1 cup (8 fl oz/250 ml) of the remaining water. Bring to a boil, then reduce the heat to low, cover, and simmer for 15 minutes.

✧ Stir in the green beans and zucchini, cover and simmer, stirring occasionally, until the vegetables are soft but still hold their shape and the grain is tender, 35–40 minutes. If the soup becomes too thick, stir in the remaining 1 cup (8 fl oz/250 ml) water. Season with salt and pepper, to taste.

✧ To serve, ladle the soup into warmed serving bowls. Drizzle each serving with a little olive oil and sprinkle with the cheese. Serve immediately.

summer
tomato and bread
soup

serves 6

When summer's tomatoes are at their peak, Italian trattorias (casual eateries with home-style cooking) combine them with stale bread and fruity olive oil to make this flavorsome soup. To capture the true Italian character of this rustic dish, use a dense, country-style loaf of bread.

1 loaf coarse country bread

3 tablespoons extra virgin olive oil, plus extra to serve

2 small cloves garlic, thinly sliced

5–5½ lb (2.5–2.75 kg) ripe plum (Roma) or beefsteak tomatoes, peeled, seeded, and chopped

1 fresh sage leaf, finely chopped

½ teaspoon finely chopped fresh basil

salt and ground black pepper

3–4 cups (24–32 fl oz/750 ml–1 liter) vegetable or meat stock

2 teaspoons red wine vinegar

❀ Trim the crusts from the bread and cut the bread into 1-inch (2.5-cm) cubes; you should have about 8 oz (250 g). Place in a single layer on a tray and set aside, uncovered, overnight.

❀ Heat the olive oil in a deep, heavy-based saucepan over low heat. Add the garlic and stir for 1 minute. Add the bread and cook, stirring, for 2 minutes; do not let it brown. Add the tomatoes and cook, stirring occasionally, until they begin to soften, about 5 minutes. Stir in the sage and basil. Season to taste with salt and pepper.

❀ As the bread absorbs the tomatoes, add some of the stock, as needed, to keep the mixture soupy. At the same time, use a spoon to mash the bread so the soup is thick and the bread blends into the tomato sauce.

❀ Cook, stirring occasionally, until thickened and no chunks of bread remain, 30–40 minutes. Remove from the heat and set aside for 30–60 minutes to let the flavors blend and develop.

❀ Return the pan to low heat and stir in the vinegar. Bring to a simmer and simmer until the sharp fumes of the vinegar have evaporated, about 1 minute. Taste and adjust the seasoning, if necessary. Ladle into warmed serving bowls and serve drizzled with a little olive oil.

soups *with* legumes

bean, potato, and sauerkraut soup

serves 4–6

8 oz (250 g) fresh, or 4 oz (125 g) dried, cranberry (borlotti) beans

4–5 potatoes, peeled

1 celery stalk

1 large onion

2 cloves garlic

2 bay leaves

3 oz (90 g) prosciutto, fat trimmed and reserved

1 tablespoon all-purpose (plain) flour

8 oz (250 g) drained sauerkraut

salt and ground black pepper

3 tablespoons olive oil

pinch of ground cumin

❖ If using dried beans, soak for 12 hours; drain.

❖ Place the beans, potatoes, celery, onion, 1 garlic clove, 1 bay leaf, and half of the prosciutto in a large pot. Add water to cover by 2 inches (5 cm). Bring to a boil, then reduce heat and simmer for 1½ hours.

❖ Meanwhile, heat the prosciutto fat in a small frying pan. Add the flour and stir until browned. Remove fat.

❖ Squeeze the moisture from the sauerkraut. Place in a saucepan with the remaining garlic, bay leaf, and prosciutto. Stir in the browned flour, salt, pepper, and enough water to cover. Cook slowly for 1 hour.

❖ Process 3 ladlefuls of the soup mixture until smooth. Return to the pan and stir in the sauerkraut mixture. Cook for 30 minutes more. Adjust the seasoning. Stir in the olive oil and cumin. Serve warm rather than hot.

genoese minestrone with pesto

serves 4–6

This is a very simple minestrone that is rich in garden vegetables, with the all-important addition of a spoonful of pesto just before serving. Adding this strongly flavored Genoese sauce to the soup gives it a character all of its own.

2 oz (60 g) dried cranberry (borlotti) beans

2 oz (60 g) dried cannellini beans

2 zucchini (courgettes), diced

2 small eggplants (aubergines), diced

3 tomatoes, peeled, seeded, and diced

1 bunch celery, trimmed and diced

2 potatoes, peeled and diced

2 tablespoons olive oil

1½ tablespoons coarse (kosher) salt

5 oz (155 g) pasta (such as broken-up spaghetti, shells, macaroni, penne, or other short pasta)

2 tablespoons basil pesto (recipe at right)

Soak the cranberry and cannellini beans for 12 hours in cold water. Drain well. Combine the beans, vegetables, olive oil, and salt in a large saucepan. Add enough cold water to cover. Bring to a boil, then reduce the heat to medium-low, cover, and cook for about 1 hour, or until the beans are tender.

Stir in the pasta, increase the heat to medium-high, and cook until the pasta is al dente. Remove from the heat, add the pesto, and stir with a wooden spoon. Serve immediately.

basil pesto

2 bunches fresh basil
3 tablespoons pine nuts
2 cloves garlic
1 tablespoon grated pecorino romano cheese
1 tablespoon grated Parmesan cheese
2 cups (16 fl oz/500 ml) extra virgin olive oil
salt

Immerse the basil in boiling water for 1 minute (this will give a lovely, bright-green pesto that will not darken). Wash and dry the leaves, then shred them by hand. Place in a mortar with the pine nuts and garlic and pound with a pestle until the mixture forms a paste. Add the cheeses and oil, a little at a time, pounding constantly and alternating the pecorino romano and Parmesan. Make sure that each addition is absorbed before adding more.

As the mixture thickens, add a little more oil. When all is incorporated, taste and add salt, if needed. The pesto should be a creamy and soft sauce. (This recipe may also be made using a food processor; the order of procedure is the same.)

preparing grains and legumes

Grains and legumes (a collective term for dried beans, peas, and lentils) are appreciated the world over and play an important role in the diet, supplying protein, carbohydrates, vitamins, and minerals.

Grains are the seed kernels of cereal plants belonging to the grass family. Most require some processing, such as husking or polishing, after harvesting to make them easier to cook and digest. Whole grains are those that retain the complete kernel— bran, oil-rich germ, and endosperm. Grains in these forms take longer to cook and can turn rancid if not stored in a cool, dry place.

preparing grains

Most grains should be rinsed before cooking to remove any foreign matter or dust that remains after processing. Unless the recipe states otherwise, grains usually do not need to be soaked before cooking.

cooking grains

Bring a measured amount of water to a vigorous boil in a saucepan. (Be sure to use a large enough pan; during cooking, grains expand to up to four times their original size.) Add seasoning, if called for, then the grain. Stir once with a wooden spoon, cover, and reduce heat to low.

At the end of the suggested cooking time, uncover; if all liquid has been absorbed and the grain is tender, it is ready to eat. If mixture looks soupy, cook for a little longer. Depending ion the grain, cooking time varies from 20–50 minutes.

After cooking, let the grain sit, covered, for about 5 minutes. Remove the lid and fluff with a fork to separate the grains and make them easier to serve.

preparing legumes

With the exception of lentils, dried legumes must be soaked before cooking. Whichever method you use—overnight soaking or quick soaking—first place the beans in a fine-meshed sieve and rinse well under cold running water, tossing to wet all the legumes. Remove and discard any damaged or discolored beans or foreign material such as sticks or pebbles. Then soak as described below. If the room is warm, let the beans soak for 8 hours or overnight in the refrigerator, or quick soak for 1 hour.

quick soaking Cover the beans with at least 3 times their volume of water and bring to a boil. Reduce heat and simmer, uncovered, for 2 minutes. Remove from heat, cover, and set aside for 1 hour. Drain off the soaking liquid and rinse, then cook as directed. If using dried red kidney beans, boil them for 10 minutes before cooking.

overnight soaking Put the beans in a large pot. Fill the pot with enough cold water to cover the beans by about 2 inches (5 cm) or according to the recipe. Cover and set aside in a cool place for 8 hours or overnight. The beans will absorb most of the water and will expand and look plump.

cooking legumes

After soaking, drain beans in a colander and rinse well. Cook beans until they are soft, or as directed in the recipe. Taste a bean, or pick one up and squeeze it with your thumb and index finger to see if it is tender. If it is still firm in the center, cook a little longer.

pasta with chickpeas

serves 6

10 oz (315 g) dried chickpeas (garbanzo beans), soaked in cold water for 24 hours

3 fresh sage leaves, chopped

pinch of coarse (kosher) salt

2½ cups (10 oz/315 g) all-purpose (plain) flour

2 eggs

½ cup (4 fl oz/125 ml) lukewarm water, or as needed

1 cup (1½ oz/45 g) finely chopped fresh parsley, for garnishing

meat or vegetable extract (optional)

1 cup (8 fl oz/250 ml) extra virgin olive oil

◈ Drain and rinse the chickpeas. Place in a saucepan and add enough cold water to cover. Add the sage and salt. Cover and cook over medium heat for 2 hours.

◈ Meanwhile, place the flour in a bowl. Mix in the eggs and as much lukewarm water as necessary to form a dough. Roll out the dough into a thin sheet and cut into large, irregular, rectangular pasta shapes.

◈ Drain chickpeas, reserving the cooking liquid. Boil the liquid until it reduces a little. Taste and add meat or vegetable extract to improve the flavor, if required.

◈ Return the chickpeas to the liquid and bring to a boil. Add the pasta and cook for 5–7 minutes, or until al dente. Serve immediately, sprinkled with chopped parsley and drizzled with extra virgin olive oil.

pasta, lentil, and pepperoni soup

serves 6

6 1/2 oz (200 g) red lentils

4 cups (32 fl oz/1 liter) chicken stock

1 bay leaf

1 tablespoon olive oil

1 large onion, finely chopped

1 can (14 1/2 oz/455 g) tomatoes, roughly chopped

8 oz (250 g) small tubular pasta or similar short pasta

6 1/2 oz (200 g) pepperoni, thinly sliced

✧ Place the lentils, stock, and bay leaf in a large saucepan. Bring to a boil, then reduce the heat and simmer for 1–1 1/4 hours, or until the lentils are very soft. Place the mixture in a food processor and process until smooth. Return to the pan.

✧ Heat the olive oil in a frying pan. Add the onion and cook, stirring often, until it is soft. Add the cooked onion and the undrained tomatoes to the soup and simmer gently for 15 minutes.

✧ Meanwhile, cook the pasta in a large saucepan of boiling salted water until al dente. Drain and stir into the soup with the pepperoni.

✧ Heat through, then serve immediately.

the virtues

serves 6

6 oz (185 g) mixed dried legumes (such as
chickpeas/garbanzo beans, lentils, and
cannellini beans), soaked for 24 hours

1 chicory (curly endive), trimmed
and thinly sliced

1 bunch beet (beetroot) greens, thinly sliced

1 celery stalk, thinly sliced

2 carrots, peeled and thinly sliced

3 oz (90 g) spinach leaves, thinly sliced

6 oz (185 g) pork rind

3 oz (90 g) prosciutto

1 pig's trotter (foot)

1 pig's ear

1 sprig fresh marjoram

1 sprig fresh mint

1½ oz (45 g) pork fat, chopped

1 tablespoon chopped fresh parsley

1 small onion

2 cloves garlic

1 small piece fresh chile

3 ripe tomatoes, peeled,
seeded, and chopped

8 oz (250 g) shelled green peas

8 oz (250 g) shelled fava (broad) beans

grated pecorino romano cheese, to serve

8 oz (250 g) broken-up spaghetti or
bucatini, cooked (optional)

❖ Cook the drained mixed legumes in boiling salted water for about 1 hour, or until tender; drain.

❖ Meanwhile, in another saucepan cook the chicory, beet greens, celery, carrots, and spinach in a small amount of salted water until just tender.

❖ In a third saucepan, boil the pork rind, prosciutto, pig's trotter, and pig's ear in enough water to cover. When they are cooked, remove the bones, finely chop the meat, and return it to the cooking liquid. Add the legumes and the marjoram and mint leaves.

❖ Brown the pork fat in a wide, shallow frying pan with the parsley, onion, garlic, chile, and tomatoes. Add to the meat mixture with the cooked vegetables. Stir in the peas and fava beans and cook until the peas and beans are tender.

❖ Serve immediately, sprinkled with cheese. For a heartier dish, stir in the cooked pasta, if desired.

food fact

This Italian soup is so named because its ingredients are supposed to be the same in number as the (purely hypothetical) virtues of a perfect mistress of the house: love of family, love of her children, fidelity, wisdom in the management of the home, and so on.

pasta and bean soup

soup

serves 4–6

Of all the Italian soups, this is certainly the most famous, and is common to a number of regions. Almost all are made by this method, in which the beans are cooked first, then some of them are puréed to increase the density of the broth, and the pasta is added at the end.

10 cups (2½ qt/2.5 l) water

2 lb (1 kg) fresh cranberry (borlotti) beans, or 5 oz (155 g) dried borlotti beans soaked in cold water overnight and drained

salt and ground black pepper

4 ripe tomatoes, peeled and seeded

1½ cups (12 fl oz/375 ml) olive oil, plus extra for drizzling

1 sprig fresh rosemary

1 tablespoon combined chopped garlic and fresh parsley leaves

5 oz (155 g) short pasta (such as penne, small rigatoni, or broken-up spaghetti)

◈ Bring the water to a boil in a large saucepan. Add the beans and a pinch of salt and cook for 1 hour.

◈ Process 2 ladlefuls of the beans with the tomatoes until smooth. Set the remaining beans aside, still in their cooking liquid.

◈ Heat 1 cup (8 fl oz/250 ml) of the olive oil in a saucepan. Add the rosemary and cook gently for 5 minutes to flavor the oil; discard the rosemary. Add the tomato mixture and garlic mixture. Stir to combine.

◈ Add the remaining beans and their cooking liquid to the pan. Stir in the pasta. Taste and adjust the seasonings, if necessary. Cook until the pasta is just al dente and the soup has a creamy consistency.

◈ Serve drizzled with olive oil, if desired.

recipe variations

Almost any type of short pasta can be used in this recipe. Alternatively, simply break up long ribbon pasta, if desired. You could also try substituting different beans, such as cannellini or great Northern (white haricot) beans.

canary island
hotpot

serves 4

12 oz (375 g) chickpeas
(garbanzo beans), soaked in
cold water overnight
and drained

16 raw almonds

2 tablespoons pine nuts

1/3 cup (2½ fl oz/80 ml) olive oil

1 onion, finely chopped
(about 5 oz/155 g)

8 oz (250 g) tomatoes,
finely chopped

2 tablespoons currants

salt

❖ Place the chickpeas in a large saucepan, add enough water to cover, bring to a boil, then reduce heat and simmer while preparing the other ingredients.

❖ Meanwhile, crush the almonds and pine nuts using a mortar and pestle.

❖ Heat the oil in a frying pan over low heat. Add the onion and cook, stirring often, until it begins to brown. Add the nuts and cook, stirring, for 1 minute. Stir in the tomatoes and currants and cook for 15 minutes.

❖ Add the tomato mixture to the chickpeas and season with a little salt. Cook over low heat for about 1 hour, or until the chickpeas are tender. Serve at once.

macaroni
and bean soup

serves 6

6½ oz (200 g) dried cannellini beans,
soaked in cold water overnight and drained

4 oz (125 g) macaroni

14 oz (440 g) speck, pancetta, or
smoked bacon, cubed

2 large onions, chopped

1 clove garlic, finely chopped

4 large tomatoes, chopped

7 cups (56 fl oz/1.75 l) vegetable stock

1 bouquet garni (1 large sprig each of
thyme, oregano, and parsley, tied together
in a square of cheesecloth/muslin)

salt and ground black pepper

2 tablespoons chopped fresh parsley (optional)

✧ Combine all the ingredients
except the parsley in a large
saucepan. Bring to a boil, then
reduce the heat and simmer for
1–1½ hours, or until the beans
are cooked through. Taste and
adjust the seasoning.

✧ Serve sprinkled with the
chopped parsley, if desired.

pinto bean soup with fresh salsa

serves 6

10 oz (315 g) dried pinto beans

7 cups (56 fl oz/1.75 l) water

¼ cup (2 fl oz/60 ml) vegetable oil

2 yellow onions, diced

1 teaspoon salt

½ teaspoon ground black pepper

4 cloves garlic, finely chopped

6 cups (48 fl oz/1.5 l) chicken stock,
vegetable stock, or water

FRESH SALSA

3 ripe plum (Roma) tomatoes, diced

½ small red (Spanish) onion, finely diced

¼ cup (⅓ oz/10 g) coarsely chopped
cilantro (fresh coriander)

juice of 1 lime

salt and ground black pepper

sour cream, to serve

Sort through the beans and discard any stones or misshapen or discolored beans. Rinse well. Place the beans in a saucepan and add the water. Bring to a boil, then reduce the heat to medium-low, cover, and simmer until the beans are cooked through and creamy inside, about 1½ hours. Remove from the heat and set aside.

Meanwhile, heat the oil in a large saucepan over medium heat. Add the onions, salt, and pepper and cook, stirring often, until the onions are lightly browned, about 10 minutes. Add the garlic and cook for 1–2 minutes more. Add the beans and their liquid and the stock or water. Bring to a boil, then reduce the heat to medium and simmer, uncovered, stirring occasionally, until the beans begin to break down, 20–30 minutes. Remove from the heat and allow to cool slightly.

Meanwhile, for the salsa, combine the tomatoes, onion, cilantro, lime juice, salt, and pepper in a bowl. Cover and refrigerate until ready to use.

Working in batches, transfer the bean mixture to a food processor and process until smooth. Transfer to a clean saucepan and reheat over low heat, stirring often, until hot. (If you are not serving the soup immediately, keep warm over very low heat, stirring often.)

Ladle the soup into warmed shallow bowls and top each serving with a spoonful of the salsa and a dollop of sour cream.

lentil stew

serves 4

10 oz (315 g) green or
brown lentils

2 tablespoons olive oil

1 onion, chopped

2 oz (60 g) pancetta,
finely chopped

5–6 fresh sage leaves

1 clove garlic, chopped

salt

❖ Soak the lentils overnight in plenty of cold water. Drain and rinse well.

❖ Heat the olive oil in a saucepan over medium-low heat. Add the onion, pancetta, sage, and garlic and cook, stirring often, for 3 minutes. Do not let the garlic brown. Add the lentils and enough water to cover. Season with salt, cover, and cook over low heat for 1 hour or until the lentils are very soft.

❖ Serve with crusty Italian bread, if desired, or as an accompaniment to cooked meats.

tagliatelle
and chickpea soup

serves 4

8 oz (250 g) dried chickpeas
(garbanzo beans), soaked
in cold water overnight
and drained

salt

5 oz (155 g) tagliatelle

¼ cup (2 fl oz/60 ml)
olive oil

1 large onion, finely chopped

2 cloves garlic, finely chopped

1 large sprig fresh rosemary

2 teaspoons tomato paste

❖ Place the chickpeas in a large saucepan with enough water to cover. Add a pinch of salt. Bring to a boil, then reduce the heat and simmer until tender, about 1 hour.

❖ Place two-thirds of the chickpeas in a food processor with their cooking liquid. Process until smooth.

❖ Meanwhile, in a large saucepan of boiling salted water cook the pasta until al dente.

❖ Heat the olive oil in a frying pan. Add the onion, garlic, and rosemary, and cook, stirring often, until the onion softens. Stir in the tomato paste. Add the puréed chickpeas, onion mixture, and pasta to the whole chickpeas and stir to combine. Heat through.

❖ Remove the sprig of rosemary and serve immediately.

baked beans

serves 6 as an accompaniment

Dried beans saw early American settlers through many a long, cold winter. Nonperishable, protein-rich, and flavorsome, baked beans have been both a necessity and a favorite for generations. These beans are even better reheated the following day. Serve them with hamburgers or grilled hot dogs.

1 lb (500 g) dried small white (navy) or great Northern (white haricot) beans

1 yellow onion, coarsely chopped

¼ cup (3 oz/90 g) dark molasses (molasses)

2 tablespoons packed light brown sugar

1 tablespoon dry mustard

1 tablespoon Worcestershire sauce

½ cup (4 fl oz/125 ml) apple cider

2 tablespoons bourbon whiskey

¼ cup (2 fl oz/60 ml) tomato purée

½ teaspoon salt

¼ teaspoon ground black pepper

1 cup (8 fl oz/250 ml) water

8 oz (250 g) ham, preferably honey-baked, diced

❧ Sort through the beans and discard any stones or misshapen or discolored beans. Rinse well. Place in a bowl, add enough water to cover by 2 inches (5 cm), and soak overnight. Drain.

❧ Bring a large saucepan of water to the boil. Add the beans and onion to the boiling water and return the water to a boil. Reduce the heat to medium-low, cover partially, and simmer until the beans and onion are very tender, 1–1½ hours. Drain well and set aside.

❧ Preheat an oven to 350°F (180°C/Gas Mark 4). In a saucepan over medium heat combine the molasses, brown sugar, mustard, Worcestershire sauce, apple cider, whiskey, tomato purée, salt, pepper, and water. Bring to a simmer, stirring until the sugar dissolves. Simmer for a few minutes more to blend the flavors.

❧ In a 6-cup (48 fl oz/1.5-l) baking dish, combine the bean mixture and the sauce. Add a little more water if the mixture looks dry. Stir in the ham. Cover and bake for 35 minutes. Uncover and increase the temperature to 400°F (200°C/Gas Mark 5). Continue baking until the liquid is almost completely absorbed, 45–60 minutes.

❧ Serve immediately, or allow to cool, then cover and refrigerate overnight. To reheat, return the baked beans to room temperature, then place in an oven preheated to 375°F (190°C/Gas Mark 4) until heated through, about 25 minutes.

chickpea and spinach
hotpot

serves 4

This hearty Spanish soup is
very popular in Madrid, and
is made of a combination of
chickpeas (garbanzo beans),
potato chunks, spinach,
eggs, and toasted bread in
a delicious broth.

1 lb (500 g) chickpeas (garbanzo beans),
soaked in cold water overnight, and drained

2 lb (1 kg) spinach, washed and chopped

1 lb (500 g) potatoes, peeled and cut into chunks

salt

2 hard-boiled eggs

¾ cup (6 fl oz/180 ml) olive oil

1 thick slice French bread (about 1 oz/30 g)

2 cloves garlic, peeled

1 onion, finely chopped

1 teaspoon paprika

◈ Bring a large saucepan of water to a boil. Add the chickpeas, cover, and cook over low heat until almost tender, about 1 hour.

◈ Stir in the spinach, potatoes, and salt and cook slowly for 30 minutes more.

◈ Chop the whites of the eggs. Reserve the yolks.

◈ Heat the oil in a frying pan. Add the slice of bread and cook until browned on both sides. Remove from the pan and set aside. Add the garlic to the pan and stir until fragrant but not browned. Remove and set aside. Add the onion to the pan and cook, stirring often, until it begins to brown. Stir in the paprika, then quickly add to the chickpea mixture. Place the garlic, bread, and egg yolks in a mortar and pound with a pestle. Add to the chickpea mixture along with the chopped egg white and stir to combine.

◈ Taste and adjust the seasoning, if necessary. Cook slowly for 15 minutes more, or until the chickpeas are tender. Serve immediately.

recipe hint

Chickpeas, also known as garbanzo beans, are one of the most versatile legumes. Hummus (a cold purée often served as a dip) and falafels (fried balls or patties) both use chickpeas as their main ingredient. Chickpeas can be boiled, roasted, sprouted, or ground into flour.

alto aragon
lentil hotpot

serves 4

12 oz (375 g) brown lentils

1 ham bone

1/3 cup (2 1/2 fl oz/80 ml) olive oil

2 leeks, washed, chopped

1 onion (5 oz/155 g), chopped

1 tomato (4 oz/125 g),
peeled and chopped

1 blood sausage (black pudding),
about 3 1/2 oz (105 g), chopped

5 oz (155 g) fresh button
mushrooms, chopped and sprinkled
with the juice of 1/2 lemon

salt

a few drops of dry anisette liqueur

1/3 cup (2 1/2 fl oz/80 ml)
muscatel wine

◈ Bring a large saucepan of water to the boil.
Add the lentils and ham bone, return to the boil,
then reduce heat and simmer while you prepare
the other ingredients.

◈ Meanwhile, heat the oil in a frying pan. Add
the leeks and onion and cook, stirring often, until
they begin to brown. Stir in the tomato and cook
over medium heat for 10 minutes. Add the blood
sausage and mushrooms and cook, stirring often,
for 10 minutes more.

◈ When the lentils are almost ready (about
40 minutes), stir in the sausage mixture and a
little salt. Cook for 40 minutes more, then
sprinkle the lentil mixture with the anisette and
stir in the muscatel wine. Serve immediately.

fava bean
casserole

serves 4

This Spanish casserole, which combines fava (broad) beans with fresh artichokes, onions, and tomatoes, is given a special touch by the addition of a mixture of ingredients crushed in a mortar, which accentuates their contrasting flavors and aromas.

8 artichokes (about 1 lb 10 oz/815 g total weight)

4 lb (2 kg) fresh fava (broad) beans, unshelled

⅓ cup (2½ fl oz/80 ml) olive oil

1 thick slice French bread (about 1 oz/30 g)

3 green (spring) onions, finely chopped

1 clove garlic, finely chopped

2 ripe tomatoes (8 oz/250 g),
peeled and finely chopped

3 sprigs fresh mint, 3 sprigs fresh flat-leaf (Italian)
parsley and 1 bay leaf, tied together

salt

pinch of ground cumin

pinch of saffron

3 black peppercorns

4 eggs

fava bean casserole

◈ Working with 1 artichoke at a time, cut off the top half. Trim the stem until it is even with the base of the artichoke. Snap or cut off the tough outer leaves until you reach the pale-green, tender leaves. Carefully open the leaves and use a small spoon to remove the prickly choke, leaving the inner leaves intact. Cut the prepared artichokes in half.

◈ Shell the fava beans and cook in a small amount of boiling water for 10 minutes.

◈ Heat the olive oil in a frying pan. Add the bread and cook until browned on both sides. Remove and set aside. Add the green onions and garlic to the pan and cook, stirring often, until they begin to brown. Stir in the tomatoes and cook over low heat until warmed through.

◈ Drain the beans and place in a heatproof casserole. Add the tomato mixture, artichokes, the bunch of herbs, and just enough water to cover. Add a little salt, then cover and cook over low heat for 40 minutes.

◈ Meanwhile, use a mortar and pestle to crush the cumin, saffron, peppercorns, and toasted bread. Add a little cooking liquid from the casserole to dilute the mixture. Add to the casserole.

◈ Break the eggs into a cup, one at a time, and arrange them on top of the bean mixture in the casserole. Serve as soon as the eggs are set.

stick-to-your-ribs chili

serves 10–12

What makes an authentic chili, especially in the American Southwest, causes many heated discussions: beans or no beans, ground meat or chunks, mild or hot, and so on. In this version, you can replace the oil with bacon fat or lard for a more savory taste. Serve with warm corn bread (recipe page 46).

⅓ cup (2½ fl oz/80 ml) vegetable oil

4 lb (2 kg) beef chuck, coarsely ground (minced)

3 large yellow onions, finely chopped

2 fresh jalapeño chiles, seeded and finely chopped

8 cloves garlic, finely chopped

2 tablespoons ground cumin

4 teaspoons ground oregano

2 teaspoons ground coriander

1 teaspoon ground cinnamon

¼ cup (¾ oz/20 g) chile powder, or to taste

2 cans (12 fl oz/375 ml each) beer

2 cups (16 fl oz/500 ml) beef stock

1 can (28 oz/875 g) crushed tomatoes

3 cans (15 oz/470 g each) kidney or pinto beans, drained

2 teaspoons salt

stick-to-your-ribs chili

TOPPINGS

sour cream

tomato salsa or jalapeño salsa

shredded sharp Cheddar cheese

chopped green (spring) onion
or red (Spanish) onion

✧ Heat 1 tablespoon of the oil in a large nonstick frying pan. Add half of the beef and cook, stirring occasionally, until well browned, 5–7 minutes. Transfer to a colander placed over a bowl to drain off the fat. Brown the remaining meat in another tablespoon of the oil, then drain. Set aside.

✧ Heat the remaining oil in a large saucepan over medium heat. Add the onions and cook, stirring occasionally, until they soften, 5–8 minutes. Add the chiles and cook, stirring often, for 1 minute. Add the garlic, cumin, oregano, coriander, cinnamon, and chile powder and stir until well combined. Cook for a few minutes to blend the flavors.

✧ Stir in the beef, beer, stock, and undrained tomatoes and bring to a gentle simmer. Reduce the heat to medium-low, cover partially, and simmer, stirring occasionally, for 1 hour.

stick-to-your-ribs chili

✧ Stir in the beans and continue to simmer, uncovered, until the mixture thickens slightly, about 30 minutes. Add the salt and stir well.

✧ Place the sour cream, salsa, cheese, and chopped onion in small bowls to be passed separately. Serve the chili immediately in warmed serving bowls.

recipe variations

If desired, you could serve this dish with warmed flour tortillas, taco shells, or simply a loaf of crusty bread to mop up the delicious juices. If necessary, you can make this dish go even further by serving it with cooked white rice.

cuban black beans with pork

serves 6–8

Turn this hearty bean stew into a vegetarian dish by omitting the pork and cooking the vegetables in the oil. Serve with a green salad with red (Spanish) onion and orange slices for a colorful Cuban-style meal.

12 oz (375 g) dried black or red kidney beans, rinsed

14 cups (3½ qt/3.5 l) water

1–2 tablespoons vegetable oil

1½ lb (750 g) lean pork shoulder, cut into 1-inch (2.5-cm) pieces

1 large red (Spanish) onion, chopped

1 large red or green bell pepper (capsicum), chopped

2 cloves garlic, finely chopped

1½ cups (12 fl oz/375 ml) water

1 teaspoon salt

½ teaspoon ground cumin

¼ teaspoon crushed dried chiles

¼ teaspoon ground black pepper

✤ Place the beans and 6 cups (48 fl oz/1.5 l) of the water in a large saucepan. Bring to a boil. If using black beans, reduce the heat and simmer for 2 minutes; if using red kidney beans, boil for 10 minutes. Remove from the heat. Cover and set aside for 1 hour. (Or, omit the simmering, and soak the beans in 6 cups (48 fl oz/1.5 l) cold water in a large saucepan, covered, for 6–8 hours or overnight.) Drain the beans and rinse well.

✤ Return the beans to the pan and add the remaining 8 cups (64 fl oz/2 l) water. Bring to a boil, then reduce the heat, cover and simmer, stirring occasionally, for 1–2 hours, or until the beans are tender.

✤ Meanwhile, in a deep, 12-inch (30-cm) frying pan, heat 1 tablespoon of the oil. Add half of the pork and cook, turning often, until well browned all over. Use a slotted spoon to remove from the pan. Brown the remaining pork, adding more oil if necessary. Remove from the pan. Add the onion, bell pepper, and garlic and cook, stirring often, for 3 minutes. Drain off the excess oil. Return the pork to the pan. Add the 1½ cups (12 fl oz/375 ml) water, the salt, cumin, chiles, and pepper. Bring to a boil, then reduce the heat, cover, and simmer for about 1 hour, or until the pork is very tender.

✤ Drain the beans and mash slightly. Stir into the pork mixture. Cook, stirring occasionally, for about 5 minutes more, or until the mixture thickens slightly. Serve.

lamb cassoulet

serves 6

A cassoulet is a hearty bean
dish native to southwestern
France. Traditionally, it
contains several kinds of
meat, including lamb, duck,
or sausage, but this
simplified version uses only
boned lamb and vegetables.

8 oz (250 g) dried great Northern (white haricot)
or cannellini beans, rinsed

4 cups (32 fl oz/1 liter) water

2 tablespoons oil

1½ lb (750 g) boned lamb, cut into bite-sized cubes

1 large onion, chopped

2 cloves garlic, finely chopped

1½ cups (12 fl oz/375 ml) chicken or beef stock

2 bay leaves

2 sprigs fresh parsley

1 teaspoon dried basil, crushed

1 teaspoon dried marjoram, crushed

½ teaspoon salt

¼ teaspoon ground black pepper

4 oz (125 g) sliced peeled carrot

1 lb (500 g) canned diced tomatoes, with juice

½ cup (4 oz/125 ml) dry white wine

In a large saucepan combine the beans and water. Bring to a boil, then reduce the heat and simmer for 2 minutes. Remove from the heat, cover, and set aside for 1 hour. Drain and rinse.

Heat the oil in a large saucepan. Add half of the lamb and cook, turning often, until browned all over. Remove from the pan. Add the remaining lamb, onion, and garlic. Cook, stirring often, until the lamb is browned. Drain excess fat. Stir in the beans, cooked lamb, stock, bay leaves, parsley, basil, marjoram, salt, and pepper. Bring to a boil, then reduce heat, cover, and simmer for 1 hour.

Stir in the carrot and cook, stirring occasionally, for 30 minutes, or until the lamb and beans are tender. Add water to the pan, if necessary, to keep the beans moist. Remove the bay leaves and parsley. Stir in the undrained tomatoes and wine and simmer, covered, for 15 minutes more. Serve immediately.

recipe hint

If desired, you can omit the initial simmering of the beans. Instead, soak the beans in 4 cups (32 fl oz/ 1 liter) of cold water for 6–8 hours or overnight. Drain and rinse the beans, and continue with the recipe.

soups *with* fish *and* seafood

fish stock

makes 5 cups (40 fl oz/1.25 l)

1 tablespoon sweet
(unsalted) butter

2 lb (1 kg) cod, halibut or
haddock steaks

6 oz (185 g) uncooked shrimp
(green prawns) or scallops

1 celery stalk, cut in half

2 thick slices yellow onion

1 cup (8 fl oz/250 ml) fruity
Italian white wine

5 cups (40 fl oz/1.25 l)
cold water

1 bay leaf

½ teaspoon fresh thyme leaves
or ¼ teaspoon dried thyme

8 fresh parsley sprigs

◈ Melt the butter in a large saucepan over medium heat. Add the fish and shrimp or scallops and cook, stirring often, until opaque, 2–3 minutes.

◈ Stir in the celery, onion, and wine. Bring to a boil over high heat and boil for 1 minute. Add the water and return to a boil. Use a slotted spoon to skim any scum from the surface. Add the bay leaf, thyme, and parsley sprigs. Reduce the heat to low and simmer, uncovered, for 20 minutes.

◈ Strain the stock through a fine-mesh sieve lined with cheesecloth (muslin) into an airtight container. Use immediately, or allow to cool, cover and refrigerate for up to 12 hours or freeze for up to 2 weeks.

lobster *stew*

This rich, luscious stew is Spanish in origin. The lobsters are cooked separately, then combined with a garlic, onion, and tomato sauce. Live lobsters should be killed by anesthetizing them in the freezer before using. However, they should not be frozen.

2 medium spiny rock lobsters (about 2 lb/1 kg each)

pinch of sea salt

¾ cup (6 fl oz/180 ml) olive oil

2 medium onions (10 oz/315 g), chopped

2 cloves garlic, finely chopped

2 ripe medium tomatoes (8 oz/250 g), peeled and chopped

4 cups (32 fl oz/1 liter) fish stock

2 tablespoons finely chopped fresh parsley

2 bay leaves

ground black pepper

◈ Bring a large saucepan of water to a boil. Add the lobsters and sea salt and cook for 8–10 minutes. Remove the lobsters and allow them to cool a little, then chop and set aside.

◈ Heat the oil in a large heatproof casserole over low heat. Add the onions and cook, stirring often, until they begin to brown. Stir in the garlic and tomatoes and cook until the mixture is almost smooth.

◈ Stir in the lobster pieces, stock, parsley, and bay leaves. Cook over high heat for 10 minutes.

◈ Season with salt and pepper, to taste. Cook over medium heat for 20 minutes more. Serve immediately.

food fact

The edible portions of lobsters are the flesh inside their tails and claws, the corals, and their greenish livers. The flesh is very lean, firm, and flavorful. Lobster can be boiled, steamed, or grilled.

Italian-style fish soup

serves 4

3 lb (1.5 kg) assorted fish and seafood, such as red mullet, octopus, scorpion fish, whiting, moray eel, cuttlefish, mussels, lobster, and squid

3 ripe tomatoes, coarsely chopped

2 onions

2 celery stalks

2 carrots

pinch of salt

2 cups (16 fl oz/500 ml) olive oil

1 sprig fresh parsley, chopped

1 small piece fresh chile, chopped

2 cloves garlic, finely chopped

1 cup (8 fl oz/250 ml) dry white wine

2 tablespoons tomato paste dissolved in ½ cup (4 fl oz/125 ml) hot water

4 slices coarse whole-grain (whole-meal) country bread, toasted

⟡ Clean and wash the seafood. Remove the heads of the larger fish and place in a saucepan with a few discarded small fish, the tomatoes, 1 onion, 1 celery stalk, 1 carrot, the salt, and some cold water. Cook over medium-low heat for at least 30 minutes, or until the liquid is fairly thick. Strain through a fine-mesh sieve into a clean pan and keep warm. Discard solids.

⟡ Meanwhile, peel the remaining carrot. Thinly slice the carrot and remaining onion and celery stalk. Heat the oil in a large heatproof casserole. Add the sliced carrot, onion, and celery and cook, stirring often, until softened. Stir in the parsley, chile, and garlic and let the flavors blend. Cut the squid and cuttlefish into strips (if using). Add to the casserole and cook until their liquid evaporates. Stir in the wine and cook until evaporated. Add the tomato paste mixture, then the fish, then mussels and lobster (if using). Cook, covered, over medium heat for 15 minutes.

⟡ Meanwhile, place a slice of toast in each serving dish, or place all of the bread in a soup tureen. Ladle the fish stock over the bread. Use a slotted spoon to lift the fish and seafood from the casserole and arrange on top of the bread. Drizzle with the cooking juices and serve.

shrimp and onion soup

serves 6–8

This soup combines both French and Mexican elements. As in French onion soup, the onions are cooked gently in butter until very tender, but here the shrimp (prawns) and chiles are the main flavorings, and chicken and shrimp stock are used instead of beef stock.

4 cups (32 fl oz/1 liter) water

¼ onion

2 cloves garlic, unpeeled

½ bay leaf

1 sprig fresh thyme leaves or 1 pinch dried thyme

1 teaspoon salt, or to taste

2 lb (1 kg) uncooked shrimp (green prawns), unpeeled

3 tablespoons butter

3 onions, halved and thinly sliced

1 tablespoon all-purpose (plain) flour

2 cups (16 fl oz/500 ml) chicken stock

1–2 canned chipotle chiles

⬧ Bring the water to a boil in a medium saucepan. Add the ¼ onion, garlic, bay leaf, thyme, and salt and simmer for 20 minutes. Add the shrimp and simmer for 3 minutes more. Pour the stock through a fine-mesh sieve into a bowl. Reserve the shrimp and discard the remaining solids. Peel the shrimp.

⬧ Melt the butter in a large saucepan over low heat and cook the sliced onions, stirring occasionally, for 25 minutes, or until tender. Add the flour and stir for 2–3 minutes. Add the reserved shrimp stock and the chicken stock to the pan. Stir to combine.

⬧ Add the shrimp and chiles to the pan and simmer for 3 minutes. Serve immediately.

recipe hint

If you prefer a less spicy flavor, you can add the chiles just before serving. Or, reduce the amount of chiles or omit them altogether. Any type of chiles may be used, whether fresh, canned, or dried.

choosing and storing
fish & seafood

buying

For the best-quality fish, seek out a
reputable fishmonger or the seafood
department of a well-stocked food store
with frequent turnover. All fish should look
moist and bright and have a clean, fresh
scent. Steer clear of any that shows
discoloration, dryness, or even a hint of a
bad aroma. Whole fish, in general, should
look almost alive, with clear eyes; bright,
intact skin and scales; and red, moist gills.

Frozen fish can also be excellent, if they
were frozen on board the ship, soon after
being caught. Avoid any that look dry,
indicating freezer burn, or that come in
packages containing liquid that has frozen,
a sign of defrosting and refreezing—a
process that damages the fish's texture.

storing

Refrigerate fresh fish the moment you get
it home, and, ideally, cook it the day you
buy it. To keep it in good condition to
cook it the following day, refrigerate the
wrapped package in any container large
enough to hold it and cover it with ice.
Do not let the flesh of the fish touch the
ice, or it will cause freezer burn and leach
out flavor. Always protect the flesh with
plastic or some kind of barrier. Whole fish
may sit directly in ice with no deterioration.

Frozen fish will keep well for 1–2 months
in a freezer with a maximum temperature
of 0°F (-18°C). To defrost frozen fish, leave
it on a tray or a plate, covered, in the
refrigerator for 24 hours, then store in a
pan or tray of ice until ready to cook.

fish, asparagus, and pea casserole

1 bunch thin green asparagus

1 cup (6 oz/185 g) green peas

2 lb (1 kg) cod fillets or other firm white fish fillets

1 cup (8 fl oz/250 ml) dry white wine

1 cup (8 fl oz/250 ml) light (single) cream

salt and ground white pepper

2 teaspoons chopped fresh dill or parsley

1 cup (6 oz/185 g) canned clams or fresh cooked clam meat (optional)

❖ Cut the asparagus into 2-inch (5-cm) lengths and cook in a saucepan of boiling lightly salted water for 4 minutes; use a slotted spoon to transfer to a plate. Return the water to the boil and cook the peas until almost tender; drain.

❖ Meanwhile, cut the fish into 2-inch (5-cm) pieces and place in a casserole. Add the wine, cover and simmer gently for 6 minutes.

❖ Add the asparagus, peas, cream, salt, and pepper to the casserole. Simmer gently for 3–4 minutes, then stir in the parsley or dill and clams. Taste and adjust the seasonings, if necessary. Serve with boiled potatoes or rice, if a heartier meal is desired.

soup with fried dumplings

serves 6–8

8 oz (250 g) uncooked shrimp
(green prawns), peeled, deveined,
and finely chopped

2 oz (60 g) pork fillet, ground (minced)

1 oz (30 g) cooked pork fat,
ground (minced)

2 oz (60 g) bamboo shoots, finely chopped

1½ teaspoons salt

1 teaspoon pepper

¼ teaspoon sesame oil

1 teaspoon cornstarch (cornflour)

4 cups (32 fl oz/1 liter) peanut oil

2 tablespoons chopped cilantro
(fresh coriander)

½ cup plus 1 tablespoon water
(5 fl oz/155 ml)

1 cup (4 oz/125 g) tang (gluten-free flour)
or Chinese dumpling flour

2 teaspoons cornstarch (cornflour), extra

½ teaspoon lard

4 cups (32 fl oz/1 liter) chicken stock

1 tablespoon light soy sauce

1 teaspoon Chinese rice wine

❖ Combine the shrimp, pork, pork fat, bamboo shoots, salt, ½ teaspoon of the pepper, sesame oil, and cornstarch in a bowl. Heat 1 tablespoon of the peanut oil in a wok or frying pan over medium heat. Add the shrimp mixture and stir for 1½ minutes. Remove and set aside. When the mixture cools, stir in the cilantro.

❖ Bring the water to a rapid boil in a saucepan. Mix together the flour and cornstarch, and add to the water. Remove from the heat and stir until the mixture becomes transparent. Cover and set aside for 5 minutes. Remove the mixture from the pan and knead, adding the lard a little at a time. Continue kneading until the dough is firm.

❖ Roll the dough into a long log. Pull off about 1½ teaspoons of the dough and press with the side of a lightly greased cleaver to form a wrapper, 2 inches (5 cm) in diameter. Cover with a kitchen towel. Repeat with the remaining dough.

❖ Place about 1 tablespoonful of the shrimp mixture in the center of a wrapper. Fold the wrapper over to enclose the shrimp mixture and press the edges to form a crescent shape. Repeat with the remaining shrimp mixture and wrappers.

❖ Heat the remaining oil in the wok until very hot. Add the dumplings and lower the heat to medium-high. Fry the dumplings until golden brown. Remove, drain, and cover to keep warm.

❖ Meanwhile, bring the stock to a boil in a saucepan. Stir in the soy sauce and rice wine. Place the dumplings in serving bowls and ladle the hot soup over the top.

stewed clams
with sausage, ham, and tomatoes

2½ lb (1.25 kg) small clams in the shell

2 tablespoons olive oil

3 yellow or red (Spanish) onions, thinly sliced

4 cloves garlic, finely chopped

1½ tablespoons dried chile flakes or 2 small fresh red chiles, seeded and finely chopped (optional)

1 bay leaf, crumbled

4 oz (125 g) smoked ham or prosciutto, diced

4 oz (125 g) chorizo or other spicy sausage, casing removed, crumbled

½ cup (4 fl oz/125 ml) dry white wine

1 can (12 oz/375 g) chopped tomatoes

½ cup (¾ oz/20 g) chopped fresh flat-leaf (Italian) parsley

ground black pepper

lemon wedges

Discard any clams that do not close when lightly touched. Scrub the clams under cold running water. Place in a bowl of water, and refrigerate until needed.

Heat the olive oil in a large saucepan over medium heat. Add the onions and cook, stirring often, until tender, about 15 minutes. Add the garlic and chile flakes (if using) and stir for 3 minutes. Add the fresh chiles (if using), the bay leaf, ham or prosciutto, sausage, wine, and tomatoes. Stir well and simmer, uncovered, over low heat for 25 minutes.

Add the clams, hinges down, and cover the pan. Increase the heat to high and cook until the clams open, 3–5 minutes. Discard any that have not opened.

Sprinkle with parsley and plenty of black pepper. Serve hot, with lemon wedges and chile pepper sauce (recipe above right).

chile pepper sauce

½ cup (2 oz/60 g) coarsely chopped fresh red chiles

3 cloves garlic, finely chopped

1 teaspoon coarse (kosher) salt

1 cup (8 fl oz/250 ml) olive oil

¼ cup (2 fl oz/60 ml) red wine vinegar (optional)

Combine the ingredients in a jar. Cover and set aside in a cool, dark place for at least 1 week or for up to 1 month. Shake well before using.

makes about 1½ cups (12 fl oz/375 ml)

serves 4–6

*1 crab, about 12 oz (375 g),
or 7 oz (220 g) drained
canned crabmeat*

1 tablespoon peanut oil

*1 tablespoon shredded
fresh ginger*

*3 cups (24 fl oz/750 ml)
Secondary Broth
(pages 158–159)*

*1 can (13½ oz/420 g)
creamed corn (sweetcorn)*

*1 tablespoon chopped
cilantro (fresh coriander)*

1 teaspoon Chinese rice wine

❖ If using a fresh crab, place it, belly up, on a work surface and cut it in half. Clean thoroughly, then place in a saucepan and steam for 15 minutes. Remove the meat from the shell and set aside. Discard the shell.

❖ Heat the oil in a large saucepan and add the ginger. When the ginger is fragrant, add the broth and corn, stirring to combine. Bring the mixture to a boil, add the crabmeat, and stir well. When the soup returns to a boil, stir in the cilantro and rice wine. Serve immediately.

crabmeat
and corn soup

seafood bouillabaisse with pasta

serves 4

2 tablespoons olive oil

1 large onion, chopped

2 cloves garlic, finely chopped

1 small fresh red chile, finely chopped

2 cups (16 fl oz/500 ml) fish stock

1 can (28 oz/880 g) plum (Roma) tomatoes, undrained

1 cup (8 fl oz/250 ml) dry white wine

4 oz (125 g) pasta shells or other short pasta

2 tablespoons chopped fresh basil

salt and ground black pepper

16 mussels, beards removed, scrubbed

1 lb (500 g) firm white boneless fish fillets, cut into 1-inch (2.5-cm) cubes

8 uncooked jumbo shrimp (green king prawns), peeled, deveined, tails intact

❖ Heat the oil in a large saucepan. Add the onion, garlic, and chile and cook, stirring, for 4–5 minutes, or until the onion is soft. Stir in the stock, tomatoes, and wine. Bring to a boil, then reduce the heat and simmer for 25–30 minutes.

❖ Meanwhile, cook the pasta in a large saucepan of boiling salted water until al dente. Drain.

❖ Stir the basil and salt and pepper to taste into the tomato mixture. Add the mussels, cover, and cook for 2–3 minutes. Add the fish and shrimp and simmer over low heat for 2–3 minutes, or until just cooked. Discard any mussels that have not opened. Stir in the cooked pasta and allow to heat through. Serve immediately with crusty bread.

119

sea bass gumbo

serves 4

1 whole sea bass, about 3 lb (1.5 kg), cleaned, filleted, and skinned, with head and bones reserved

1/3 cup (2 1/2 fl oz/80 ml) vegetable oil

1/2 cup (2 oz/60 g) diced yellow onion

1/4 cup (1 oz/30 g) all-purpose (plain) flour

2 tablespoons diced spicy sausage

1/2 cup (2 oz/60 g) diced green bell pepper (capsicum)

1 celery stalk, diced

3 cloves garlic, sliced

1 teaspoon salt, plus extra to taste

1/2 teaspoon peppercorns

1/2 teaspoon dried thyme

1 bay leaf

4 cups (1 1/2 lb/750 g) diced plum (Roma) tomatoes

2 cups (16 fl oz/500 ml) water

2 tablespoons butter

1/4 lemon, sliced

1 teaspoon chopped fresh flat-leaf (Italian) parsley, plus 4 sprigs for garnishing

1/4 teaspoon filé powder

❖ Cover and refrigerate the bass fillets. Wash the fish head and bones in cold water, then cut the bones into large pieces and set aside.

❖ Heat ¼ cup (2 fl oz/60 ml) of the oil in a large saucepan. Add onion, flour, and sausage and stir until the flour browns, 6–8 minutes. Stir in the bell pepper, celery, garlic, 1 teaspoon salt, peppercorns, thyme, bay leaf, tomatoes, and water. Add fish head and bones and bring to a boil. Reduce heat and simmer, uncovered, for 1 hour, occasionally skimming scum from surface.

❖ During final 10 minutes of cooking, prepare the bass: Cut into 4 pieces and season with salt. Heat the butter and remaining oil in a large frying pan. Add fish and cook for 4 minutes. Turn and cook until fish is opaque, 4–5 minutes.

❖ Remove the gumbo from the heat. Discard fish head and bones. Strain into a small saucepan, pressing on the solids to extract liquid. Add the lemon and parsley, then stir in the filé powder.

❖ To serve, ladle gumbo into bowls, top with a piece of fish, and garnish with parsley sprigs.

121

serves 4–6

2 teaspoons salt

2 teaspoons sugar

2 teaspoons cornstarch (cornflour)

1 teaspoon sesame oil

1 tablespoon water

6 conpoy (dried sea scallops)

4 oz (125 g) uncooked shrimp (green prawns), peeled and deveined

4 oz (125 g) sea bass fillet, diced

4 cups (32 fl oz/1 liter) water

4 cups (32 fl oz/1 liter) Secondary Broth (page 158)

1 tablespoon shredded fresh ginger

2 oz (60 g) carrot, thinly sliced

1 tablespoon light soy sauce

1 teaspoon Chinese rice wine

2 tablespoons cornstarch (cornflour), dissolved in 2 tablespoons water

2 oz (60 g) cucumber, thinly sliced

1 tablespoon chopped cilantro (fresh coriander)

rainbow
seafood soup

❖ Combine the salt, sugar, cornstarch, oil, and 1 tablespoon water in a bowl. Add the conpoy, shrimp, and fish and set aside for 15 minutes to marinate.

❖ Bring the 4 cups (32 fl oz/1 liter) water to a boil in a large saucepan and add the seafood mixture. Return to a boil, then remove the seafood with a slotted spoon. Discard the cooking liquid.

❖ Bring the broth to a boil in a separate large saucepan. Add the ginger and carrot and cook for 2 minutes. Add the seafood and return the broth to a boil.

❖ Add the soy sauce and rice wine. Stir in the cornstarch solution. Serve at once, sprinkled with the cucumber and cilantro.

mediterranean
scallop stew
with crostini

serves 4

1½ lb (750 g) bay or sea scallops, with roe if desired

2 tablespoons extra virgin olive oil, plus extra for brushing

1⅓ cups (4 oz/125 g) sliced leeks (white parts only)

½ cup (2 oz/60 g) thinly sliced yellow onion

6 oz (185 g) pancetta, fat trimmed, cut into thin strips

4 cloves garlic, thinly sliced, plus 1 clove garlic, cut in half

2 cups (12 oz/375 g) peeled, seeded, and chopped plum (Roma) tomatoes (fresh or canned)

1½ cups (12 fl oz/375 ml) fruity Italian white wine

5 cups (40 fl oz/1.25 l) fish stock

8 oz (250 g) fresh white mushrooms, stems discarded, sliced

4 tablespoons chopped fresh parsley

1 bay leaf

2 strips orange zest (rind), each 2 inches (5 cm) long and ½ inch (1 cm) wide

½ teaspoon fresh thyme leaves

¼ teaspoon fennel seeds

⅛ teaspoon powdered saffron

salt and ground white pepper

4 slices coarse country bread

small fresh basil leaves, for garnishing

grated Parmesan cheese, for garnishing

mediterranean scallop stew with crostini

❖ If using sea scallops, cut crosswise into ½-inch (12-mm) thick slices. Set aside.

❖ Heat the 2 tablespoons olive oil in a large saucepan or stockpot over medium heat.
Add the leeks and onion and cook, stirring, until barely translucent, about 3 minutes;
do not allow to brown. Add the pancetta and cook, stirring, for 2 minutes. Stir in the
sliced garlic and tomatoes and cook for 1 minute.

❖ Increase heat to high, add 1¼ cups (10 fl oz/310 ml) of the wine, and stir to dislodge any
browned bits on the base of the pan. Bring to a boil, then stir in the stock, mushrooms, parsley,
bay leaf, orange zest, thyme, fennel seeds, and saffron. Return to a boil, then reduce heat to
medium and simmer, uncovered, for 15–20 minutes, or until the mushrooms are cooked and
the soup has reduced and thickened slightly.

❖ Add the scallops and cook until almost opaque in the center, 2–3 minutes. Add the
remaining wine and simmer until the scallops are just opaque, about 1 minute longer. Remove
the bay leaf and season with salt and pepper to taste.

❖ Meanwhile, toast the bread until golden. Rub the cut sides of the halved garlic clove over
1 side of each piece of toast and then brush lightly with the extra olive oil.

❖ To serve, place a piece of toast, garlic-rubbed side up, in each bowl. Ladle the stew over the
toast and serve immediately, garnished with the basil leaves and Parmesan cheese.

sour fish soup

serves 6

1 whole catfish, striped bass, sea bass, or red snapper (about 2 lb/1 kg)

1 tablespoon fish sauce

¼ teaspoon ground black pepper

1 green (spring) onion, thinly sliced

FISH SOUP

1 tablespoon vegetable oil

2 shallots, thinly sliced

3 lemongrass stalks, cut into 2-inch (5-cm) lengths and crushed

6 cups (48 fl oz/1.5 l) water or chicken stock

2 oz (60 g) tamarind pulp, chopped

1 cup (8 fl oz/250 ml) boiling water

1 cup (6 oz/185 g) diced pineapple

½ cup (2½ oz/75 g) drained, sliced canned bamboo shoots

2 small fresh red chiles, seeded and thinly sliced

1 tablespoon sugar

2 tablespoons fish sauce, or to taste

2 small, firm tomatoes, cut into wedges

1 cup (2 oz/60 g) bean sprouts

salt and ground black pepper

cilantro (fresh coriander) sprigs or sliced fresh mint leaves, for garnishing

1 lime, cut into wedges

sour fish soup

◈ If the fish is not already cleaned, use a sharp knife to slit the fish open from the tiny hole in the belly to the head. Empty the cavity of all the guts and scrape away any dark blood from the backbone. Rinse the cavity very well. Using the back of a heavy knife, scrape the scales away from the fish, working from the tail toward the head. Rinse and dry the fish well.

◈ Remove the fish head and use a thin, flexible knife to carefully cut between the fillet and the backbone, working from the tail up. Remove the fish fillet, then turn the fish over and repeat to remove the remaining fillet. Reserve the fish head, bones, and any scraps. Cut the fillets into 1-inch (2.5-cm) cubes and place in a bowl with the fish sauce, pepper, and green onion. Toss gently to combine, then set aside at room temperature to marinate.

◈ For the fish soup, heat the vegetable oil in a large saucepan over medium heat. When the oil is hot, add the fish head, bones, and scraps and stir to combine. Add the shallots and lemongrass and cook gently, stirring often, until fragrant, 3–5 minutes. Do not let the mixture brown. Add the water or chicken stock and bring to a boil. Reduce the heat to low and simmer, uncovered, for 20 minutes.

◈ Meanwhile, in a small bowl soak the tamarind pulp in the boiling water for 15 minutes. Mash the tamarind pulp using the back of a fork to help it dissolve. Carefully pour the mixture through a fine-mesh sieve into another small bowl, pressing against the tamarind pulp to extract as much of the flavorful liquid as possible. Discard the pulp and set the liquid aside.

sour fish soup

❖ Pour the stock through a fine-mesh sieve into a large saucepan. Discard the contents of the sieve. Bring the stock to a boil. Stir in the tamarind liquid, pineapple, bamboo shoots, chiles, sugar, and fish sauce. Reduce the heat to medium and simmer for 1 minute. Add the tomatoes and marinated fish and continue to simmer until the fish is opaque and feels firm to the touch, 3–5 minutes. Add the bean sprouts and season with salt and pepper, to taste.

❖ Serve immediately, garnished with cilantro or mint, and accompanied by the lime wedges.

food fact

Nearly every country in Southeast Asia has its own version of sour fish soup. Loaded with fish, vegetables, and fruit, this southern Vietnamese version is herbaceous, spicy, fruity, tangy, sweet, and savory. Serve with cooked white rice, if desired.

monkfish soup
with mayonnaise

serves 4

Monkfish live in muddy waters, at the bottom of the Atlantic Ocean and the Mediterranean Sea, in particular. They have enormous flat heads that are wider than the rest of their bodies. The only edible part of the monkfish is its tail, which is often compared to lobster meat.

6½ oz (200 g) small clams

salt

13 oz (410 g) monkfish, cut into chunks

1 onion, chopped

2 bay leaves

2 tablespoons dry white wine

1 lb (500 g) potatoes, cut into ¼-inch (6-mm) slices

⅓ cup (2½ fl oz/80 ml) thick mayonnaise

1 loaf crusty French bread (4–6 thin slices per person)

◈ Wash the clams and soak them in salted cold water to release any sand.

◈ Place the monkfish in a large heatproof casserole with enough cold water to cover. Add the onion, bay leaves, and wine. Bring to a boil and then boil for 1 minute. Remove from the heat and set aside.

◈ Place the clams in a large saucepan with enough water to barely cover them. Cook over low heat until the clam shells open. Remove from the heat. Remove the clam meat from the shells and set aside. Strain and reserve the cooking liquid.

◈ Strain the monkfish mixture. Return the strained broth to the casserole and set aside. Discard the onion and bay leaves. Remove the skin and bones from the fish. Flake the flesh and place in a bowl, covered with a little of the strained clam liquid. Cover and set aside.

◈ Bring the monkfish broth to a boil. Add the potatoes and cook for 30 minutes. Use a slotted spoon to transfer the potatoes to a plate. Reserve the broth.

◈ Place the mayonnaise in a soup tureen. Gradually add the monkfish broth and the remaining clam broth, stirring with a wooden spoon to combine.

◈ Stir in the monkfish mixture, clam meat, and potatoes. Adjust the seasoning, if necessary.

◈ Toast the slices of bread and serve with the soup.

saffron
mussel stew

Although this classic stew is of Mexican origin, it has a strong Spanish influence, which is evident in the presence of saffron. The best saffron is said to come from Spain, and it is a key ingredient in Spanish paella.

2 tablespoons olive oil

2 yellow onions, cut into julienne strips

½ teaspoon salt

½ teaspoon ground black pepper

4 cloves garlic, sliced

1½ cups (12 fl oz/375 ml) dry white wine

1 fresh thyme sprig

1 teaspoon saffron threads

2½ cups (20 fl oz/625 ml) bottled clam juice or fish stock

1 cup (8 fl oz/250 ml) good-quality tomato juice

3 lb (1.5 kg) small mussels in the shells

½ cup (¾ oz/20 g) coarsely chopped fresh flat-leaf (Italian) parsley

⬧ Heat 1 tablespoon of the olive oil in a large, heavy-based saucepan over medium heat. Add half of the onions, the salt, and pepper. Cook, stirring often, until the onions are light golden, 8–10 minutes. Add the garlic and stir for 1 minute. Stir in the wine and bring to a boil. Boil until the mixture has reduced by half, about 8 minutes. Stir in the thyme, saffron, clam juice or fish stock, and tomato juice and bring to a boil. Reduce the heat to low and simmer for 10 minutes to blend the flavors. Strain the broth and discard the solids. Set aside.

⬧ Scrub the mussels under cold running water and remove their beards. Discard any mussels that do not close when lightly touched.

⬧ Place 2 large frying pans over high heat (or cook in batches if only 1 pan is available). Add 2 teaspoons of the remaining olive oil to each pan. When the oil is hot, add half of the remaining onions to each pan and cook, stirring occasionally, until they just begin to color, about 4 minutes. Add half of the mussels to each pan, spreading them out in a single layer, and cook, stirring occasionally, for 2 minutes. Divide the strained broth between the pans and bring to a boil. Reduce the heat to medium, cover and cook until the mussels open, about 3–5 minutes. Discard any mussels that do not open.

⬧ Add half of the parsley to each pan. Toss to combine and then spoon the mussels into warmed serving dishes. Divide the broth among the bowls and serve immediately.

salt cod
and leek soup

serves 4

10 oz (315 g) dried salt cod,
soaked in water for 12 hours

1/3 cup (2 1/2 fl oz/80 ml)
olive oil

4 cloves garlic, peeled

4 medium leeks, chopped

2 lb (1 kg) potatoes,
cut into chunks

salt and ground black pepper

❖ Drain the cod. Remove the skin and bones, then break the flesh into small pieces.

❖ Heat the olive oil in a heatproof casserole. Add the garlic and stir for 30 seconds. Add the leeks and cook, stirring often, for 3 minutes. Add the potatoes and cook, stirring often, until lightly browned.

❖ Add enough water to cover the vegetables and bring to a boil. Stir in the cod. Reduce the heat to low, cover and cook for 45 minutes, stirring occasionally. Taste and season with salt and pepper. Serve.

shellfish soup

serves 6

6 lb (3 kg) mixed shellfish
(such as small clams, mussels,
pipis, and scallops)

¼ cup (2 fl oz/60 ml)
extra virgin olive oil

1 clove garlic, finely chopped

1 small onion, chopped

½ cup (4 fl oz/125 ml) dry
white wine

1 lb (500 g) tomatoes, chopped

salt and ground black pepper

1 fresh chile

1 handful chopped
fresh parsley

6 slices bread, toasted

◇ Immerse the shellfish in a basin of water, while washing and brushing them under the tap. Transfer the shellfish to a frying pan. Cover and cook over medium heat until they open. Drain, reserving any cooking liquid. Discard the empty half-shells, reserving the halves with the meat attached. Strain the cooking liquid through damp cheesecloth (muslin) and set aside.

◇ Heat the oil in a frying pan. Add the garlic and onion and cook, stirring often, until browned. Stir in the strained cooking liquid, wine, tomatoes, salt, and pepper. Cook for 15 minutes, then stir in the chile. The soup should be fairly thin; add a little water if needed.

◇ Add the reserved shellfish and cook for 1 minute. Stir in the parsley. Place a slice of toast in each serving dish. Pour over the soup and serve immediately.

fish soup

serves 6

2 lb (1 kg) mussels in the shells

4 lb (2 kg) assorted firm fish fillets
(such as bass, flounder, halibut,
haddock, snapper, cod, and grouper)

salt

½ cup (4 fl oz/125 ml) olive oil

2 cups (7 oz/220 g) sliced yellow onions

1 cup (3 oz/90 g) sliced leeks, washed well

4 cloves garlic, finely chopped

2 celery stalks, chopped

1½ cups (9 oz/280 g) peeled, seeded, and
chopped tomatoes (fresh or canned)

4 sprigs fresh thyme

1 bay leaf

½ cup (¾ oz/20 g) chopped fresh
flat-leaf (Italian) parsley

1 cup (8 fl oz/250 ml) dry white wine

7 cups (56 fl oz/1.75 l) water

1 lb (500 g) uncooked shrimp (green
prawns), peeled and deveined

fresh lemon juice

ground black pepper

❖ Discard any mussels that do not close when lightly touched. Scrub the mussels under cold running water and remove their beards. Place in a bowl and refrigerate until needed.

❖ Cut the fish fillets into 2-inch (5-cm) pieces. Place on a plate, sprinkle with salt and refrigerate until needed.

❖ Heat the olive oil in a large saucepan over medium heat. Add the onions and leeks and cook, stirring often, until they are translucent, about 8 minutes. Stir in the garlic, celery, tomatoes, thyme, bay leaf, and half of the parsley. Cook, stirring often, for 2 minutes.

❖ Add the wine and water and bring the mixture to a boil over high heat. Reduce the heat to medium and simmer for 15 minutes. Stir in the salted fish pieces, cover and cook for 5 minutes. Stir in the shrimp and mussels, cover and cook until the mussels open, 3–4 minutes. Discard any mussels that have not opened.

❖ Season with lemon juice, salt, and pepper, to taste. Serve immediately, sprinkled with the remaining parsley.

lobster
in wine sauce

serves 4

Spiny lobsters, also known as sea crayfish, have become a symbol of luxury, elegance, and refinement in many countries. As a result, they are popular party or special occasion fare, probably as much for what they are seen to represent as for their taste.

2 spiny lobsters, about 1 lb (500 g) each

½ cup (3½ oz/105 g) long-grain white rice

2 tablespoons wild rice

2 tablespoons butter

1½ tablespoons peanut oil

1 shallot, finely chopped

6 large and 12 small fresh tarragon leaves

salt and ground black pepper

4 pinches of ground cayenne pepper

½ cup (4 fl oz/125 ml) crème fraîche

½ cup (4 fl oz/125 ml) sweet white muscat wine

2 slices blood orange, halved

2 slices lemon, halved

Bring a large saucepan of salted water to a boil. Add the lobsters and return the water to a boil. Reduce heat and simmer gently for 10 minutes. Remove the lobsters and refresh them under cold running water for about 2 minutes. Spread the lobsters out on a board, unrolling the tails, and set aside for at least 30 minutes to cool completely.

Remove the tails and shell the lobsters, collecting the lobster liquid as you work. Use a small spoon to take out the creamy parts and coral found in the trunk, and place them in a blender. Blend to a thin creamy consistency. Transfer to a bowl and set aside.

Discard the head and tail carapaces but keep the claws, feelers, and the cartilaginous parts of the trunk and break them up.

Preheat an oven to 400°F (200°C/Gas Mark 5).

Cook the long-grain and wild rices in boiling salted water until they are just tender; drain. Stir in the butter and transfer to a casserole. Cover and place in the oven to keep warm.

Heat the oil in a large saucepan. Add the broken-up claws, feelers, and trunk. Cook over medium heat, turning often, for 5 minutes. Add the shallot, large tarragon leaves, salt, pepper, and cayenne pepper and stir to combine.

Cook for 2 minutes, stirring constantly. Stir in the liquid from the lobster, the crème fraîche, and wine. As the mixture comes to a boil, crush the pieces of lobster shell. When it reaches a boil, cover and cook for 10 minutes.

lobster in wine sauce

❖ Strain the lobster mixture into a clean saucepan. Let the solids drain thoroughly and then discard them. Add the orange and lemon. Heat gently for 3 minutes.

❖ Divide the rice among 4 ovenproof ramekins. Cut the lobster tails into ⅛-inch (3-mm) thick rounds, and arrange on top of the rice. Coat with the sauce, and place a piece of orange and lemon on top of each. Place the ramekins in the hot oven, turn the oven off and leave them to heat for 5 minutes.

❖ Serve immediately, garnished with the remaining small tarragon leaves.

food fact

Wild rice is not a type of rice at all, but rather the seed of an aquatic grass native to the northern Great Lakes of the United States. It grows wild in that region, and has long been harvested from boats by Native Americans. It is also cultivated elsewhere in the Midwest and in Canada and California. It is blackish in color and has a pronounced flavor similar to that of hazelnuts (filberts). Wild rice is richer in protein (and more expensive) than regular rice. It may be substituted for white or brown rice in most recipes, but keep in mind that its texture is firmer and that it takes longer to cook.

cadiz fish soup

serves 4

1¼ lb (625 g) whole cleaned
white fish, sliced

2 leeks, washed,
sliced lengthwise

2 carrots, sliced crosswise

3 cups (24 fl oz/750 ml) water

¼ cup (2 fl oz/60 ml)
dry white wine

salt

¼ cup (2 fl oz/60 ml) olive oil

1 onion (6½ oz/200 g),
thinly sliced

1 orange, juiced

1 loaf crusty French bread
(4–6 thin slices per person)

⬥ Place the fish head, leeks, carrots, water, wine, and salt in a large saucepan and cook for 30 minutes to make a broth. Strain and reserve about 2 cups (16 fl oz/500 ml) of the liquid. Keep warm.

⬥ Salt the fish slices on both sides and set aside.

⬥ Heat the oil in a heatproof casserole over low heat. Add the onion and cook, stirring often, until it begins to brown. Stir in half of the warm broth and cook for about 15 minutes, or until the onion is very soft. Stir in the remaining broth and the fish. Cook over low heat for 10 minutes.

⬥ Stir in the orange juice and serve immediately with the slices of bread.

shrimp
and spinach soup

serves 8

This Mexican soup is thickened using *tortilla masa*, which is made by mixing *masa harina* (tortilla flour) and warm water to a soft dough. Epazote is a pungent herb often used in Mexican cooking. It is also known as goosefoot, pigweed, wormseed, Jerusalem oak, and pazote.

8 cups (64 fl oz/2 l) water

3 cloves garlic, unpeeled

2 thick slices onion

salt

2 lb (1 kg) uncooked shrimp (green prawns), washed

½ teaspoon peppercorns

¼ teaspoon cumin seeds

⅓ cup (1 oz/30 g) masa harina (tortilla flour)

¼ cup (2 fl oz/60 ml) warm water

1 tablespoon plus 2 teaspoons olive oil

3½ oz (105 g) spinach leaves, washed and stemmed

1 sprig fresh epazote (optional)

◈ Bring the water to a boil in a large saucepan with 1 garlic clove, 1 slice of onion, and 1 teaspoon of salt. Add the shrimp and boil for 3 minutes or until the shrimp are opaque. Strain the liquid and reserve. Discard the garlic and onion. Peel the shrimp and set aside.

◈ Heat a small frying pan and toast the peppercorns and cumin seeds. Remove and place in a blender. In the same pan, cook the remaining garlic and onion until charred on both sides. Remove from the pan. Peel the garlic, and place in the blender with the onion and ¼ cup (2 fl oz/60 ml) of the reserved cooking liquid. Blend until smooth.

◈ Mix the masa harina and warm water together to form a soft dough (*tortilla masa*) and set aside. Heat 1 tablespoon of the oil in a large saucepan over medium heat. Add the onion mixture and cook, stirring often, for 4 minutes. Meanwhile, set aside ¼ cup (2 fl oz/60 ml) of the reserved cooking liquid. Place the spinach leaves and the remaining reserved cooking liquid in a blender and blend until smooth. Add the spinach mixture and epazote (if using) to the pan. Dissolve the *tortilla masa* in the remaining ¼ cup (2 fl oz/60 ml) of reserved cooking liquid. Add to the pan with salt, to taste, and cook over low heat, stirring occasionally, for 20 minutes.

◈ Add the shrimp and cook until heated through. Serve immediately, drizzled with the remaining 2 teaspoons of olive oil.

fish and shellfish soup

2 lb (1 kg) red snapper (sea bass or red emperor), cleaned and scaled, with the head and bones reserved

1 sprig fresh thyme

1 sprig fresh oregano

1½ teaspoons salt, or to taste

6 cups (48 fl oz/1.5 l) water

8 oz (250 g) small uncooked shrimp (green prawns), unpeeled

4 dried cascabel or large guajillo chiles, 3 seeded and stemmed, and 1 whole

1 lb (500 g) tomatoes, peeled, seeded, and roughly chopped

⅓ cup (2½ fl oz/80 ml) olive oil

1 small onion, grated

1 large clove garlic, finely chopped

1 lb (500 g) squid, cleaned, tentacles removed, cut into ¼-inch (6-mm) rings

2 tablespoons masa harina (tortilla flour)

½ cup (4 fl oz/125 ml) warm water

1 small bay leaf

❖ Remove the fillets from the fish, then remove and discard the skin. Cut the fillets into 2-inch (5-cm) pieces. Set aside.

❖ Place the fish head and bones in a large saucepan with the thyme, oregano, salt, and water. Cook over medium heat for 15 minutes. Add the shrimp and cook for 3 minutes more. Remove the shrimp and peel. Strain the stock and reserve.

❖ Soak the 3 seeded chiles in hot water for about 10 minutes to soften. Drain and discard the liquid. Place the chiles in a blender with ½ cup (4 fl oz/125 ml) of the reserved stock and blend until smooth. Add the tomatoes and continue to blend until smooth.

❖ Heat the olive oil in a large saucepan over medium heat. Add the onion and garlic and cook, stirring often, for 5 minutes, or until translucent. Add the tomato mixture and cook, stirring occasionally, until the oil rises to the surface, about 10–15 minutes.

❖ Add the remaining fish stock, fish pieces, shrimp, and squid. Bring the mixture to a simmer.

❖ Mix the *masa harina* and warm water together to form a soft dough (*tortilla masa*). Add to the pan with the bay leaf and whole chile and stir to combine. Simmer over low heat, stirring occasionally, for 20 minutes. Remove and discard the bay leaf. Serve immediately.

catalan seafood stew

serves 4–6

13 oz (410 g) monkfish, cut into 4 slices

13 oz (410 g) grouper or sea bass, cut into 4 slices

13 oz (410 g) hake, cut into 4 slices

1 lb (500 g) squid, cleaned, tentacles removed, cut into thin rings

salt and ground black pepper

¾ cup (6 fl oz/180 ml) olive oil

6 raw almonds

4 scampi (Dublin Bay prawns)

4 uncooked jumbo shrimp (green king prawns)

10 oz (315 g) onion, finely chopped

3 medium tomatoes, peeled and finely chopped

⅓ cup (2½ fl oz/80 ml) dry white wine

¼ cup (2 fl oz/60 ml) Cognac

1⅔ cups (13 fl oz/410 ml) fish stock

2 cloves garlic, finely chopped

1 tablespoon finely chopped fresh parsley

2 cookies (milk arrowroot type)

16 mussels, scrubbed, debearded, steamed

◈ Preheat an oven to 400°F (200°C/Gas Mark 5).

◈ Season all of the fish and the squid with salt and pepper.

◈ Heat the oil in a frying pan. Add the almonds and cook, stirring often, until toasted. Remove from the pan and set aside. Add the scampi and shrimp and cook, stirring often, until opaque and just cooked through. Transfer to a large, shallow heatproof casserole. Add the squid to the pan and cook, stirring often, until it begins to brown. Add to the casserole.

◈ Add the fish to the pan and cook, turning occasionally, until opaque and just cooked through. Add to the casserole. Add the onion to the pan and cook, stirring often, until it begins to brown. Stir in the tomatoes and cook over high heat until heated through. Stir in the wine and Cognac and cook until the liquid is almost completely reduced. Add the fish stock and a little salt to the pan. Boil, stirring often, for 2–3 minutes, then add the mixture to the casserole.

◈ Crush the garlic and parsley using a mortar and pestle. Add the almonds and crush well. Add the cookies and crush to form a smooth paste. Stir in a little liquid from the casserole, then pour the mixture into the casserole. Add the mussels and check the seasoning.

◈ Cook over low heat, covered, for 10 minutes. Transfer to the oven and cook for 5 minutes more. Serve immediately.

bonito

casserole

This Spanish dish is particularly popular with fishermen during the bonito season and is often cooked on the boat. If bonito tuna is unavailable, you can substitute any tuna species, such as bluefin or yellowfin.

2 lb (1 kg) bonito tuna

¾ cup (6 fl oz/180 ml) olive oil

2 small onions, finely chopped

2 green bell peppers (capsicums), seeded and chopped

1 lb (500 g) potatoes, cut into chunks

salt

4 dried red bell peppers (capsicums), soaked for 12 hours, and drained

◈ Remove the skin and bones from the bonito tuna, then cut into chunks.

◈ Heat ½ cup (4 fl oz/125 ml) of the oil in a heatproof casserole. Cook the onions and green bell peppers over low heat, stirring often, until they begin to soften. Add the potatoes and cook until they begin to soften, then stir in enough water to cover. Cook for 30 minutes.

◈ Heat the remaining oil in a frying pan. Add the bonito and cook, turning often, until sealed on all sides. Add to the casserole with a little salt and cook, occasionally stirring gently, for 10 minutes.

◈ Place the red bell peppers in a blender and blend until smooth. Stir in to the casserole. Check the seasoning, then remove from the heat and set aside for a few minutes. Serve hot.

food fact

There are many species of tuna, and all tend to have long, sturdy bodies with firm flesh that is usually sold as steaks or cutlets. Tuna is also delicious when quickly seared on a griddle or barbecue, or under a broiler (griller), on both sides and left rare in the middle. Thinly sliced raw tuna is a popular ingredient in sushi and sashimi.

potato and salt cod casserole

serves 4

Potatoes and salt cod were traditionally combined to make a tasty meal for meatless days or during Lent. However, you really need no reason to enjoy this delicious dish whenever you please.

8 oz (250 g) dried salt cod, soaked overnight

1/3 cup (2 1/2 fl oz/80 ml) olive oil

1 tomato (3 1/2 oz/105 g), peeled and finely chopped

4 potatoes (about 1 lb/500 g), peeled and chopped

1 teaspoon paprika

1 tablespoon finely chopped fresh parsley

2 cloves garlic, peeled

2 teaspoons pine nuts

12 raw almonds

salt and ground black pepper

◈ Drain the cod and then break into small pieces.

◈ Heat the oil in a heatproof casserole over low heat. Add the cod and stir until coated in oil. Stir in the tomato and cook for 5 minutes. Add the potatoes and cook, turning occasionally, for 5 minutes more. Stir in the paprika. Add enough water to cover.

◈ Cook over low heat, covered, for 30–45 minutes, or until the potatoes are very tender.

◈ Crush the parsley, garlic, pine nuts, and almonds using a mortar and pestle. Stir into the casserole. Season with salt and pepper, to taste. Cook for 5 minutes more, and serve.

recipe hint

Dried, salted cod has been an important staple food in Europe and Scandinavia for centuries. Before cooking, it is necessary to soak the cod in cold water to remove the excess salt. Salt cod can be baked, broiled (grilled), fried, poached, or added to sauces, soups, and stews.

soups *with* meat

meat *stock*

1 yellow onion, unpeeled

1 chicken (3 lb/1.5 kg), cut into 8 pieces, or 3 lb (1.5 kg) chicken pieces (thighs, drumsticks, wings, and/or necks)

1 lb (500 g) beef shin (shank) with bone

8 oz (250 g) veal stew meat, cut into large cubes

1 large carrot, peeled

1 celery stalk

16 cups (4 qt/4 l) cold water

2 small pieces of rind from Parmesan cheese, about 1 oz (30 g) total weight

1 plum (Roma) tomato

❖ Preheat a broiler (griller) and broil the whole onion until the edges are lightly browned.

❖ Place the browned onion, chicken, beef, veal, carrot, and celery in a deep stockpot. Add the water and bring to a boil over high heat. Use a large slotted spoon to skim any scum from the surface. Reduce the heat to low, cover partially, and simmer for 2 hours.

❖ Add the cheese rind and tomato and simmer, uncovered, for 1 hour; do not allow mixture to boil.

❖ Remove from heat and strain through a fine-mesh sieve lined with cheesecloth (muslin) into a clean container. Use immediately, or let cool, cover, and refrigerate for up to 5 days or freeze for up to 1 month. Before using the chilled stock, lift off and discard the fat congealed on the surface.

meatball soup
with egg and lemon

serves 6

Avgolemono is the Greek term for the Mediterranean egg-and-lemon mixture used as a thickener for soups or stews. While simpler versions of this soup just include rice, the most interesting and filling interpretations feature these little meatballs.

1 lb (500 g) ground (minced) lean beef and/or lamb

1 cup (5 oz/155 g) grated or finely chopped onion

1/3 cup (2 1/2 oz/75 g) long-grain white rice or 1/2 cup (2 oz/60 g) fine dried bread crumbs

1/2 cup (2/3 oz/20 g) chopped fresh flat-leaf (Italian) parsley

2 tablespoons chopped fresh mint or dill

3 eggs

salt and ground black pepper

6 cups (48 fl oz/1.5 l) chicken stock

1/4 cup (2 fl oz/60 ml) fresh lemon juice

◈ Combine the meat, onion, rice or bread crumbs, half of the parsley, the mint or dill, and 1 of the eggs in a bowl. Season to taste with salt and pepper. Using your hands, knead the mixture until well combined. Shape into small meatballs, about ½-inch (13-mm) in diameter.

◈ Bring the stock to a boil in a large saucepan over medium-high heat. Add the meatballs, reduce the heat to low, cover, and simmer gently until meatballs are cooked, 25–30 minutes.

◈ Beat the remaining 2 eggs in a bowl until they are very frothy. Gradually beat in the lemon juice. Gradually beat in about 1½ cups (12 fl oz/375 ml) of the hot stock, beating constantly to prevent curdling. (This tempers the eggs, so they won't scramble when added to the hot stock.) Continue to beat until the mixture thickens, then slowly stir the egg mixture into the hot stock. Heat through, but do not allow the soup to boil.

◈ Serve immediately, sprinkled with the remaining parsley.

mandarin lamb

serves 4–6

1 lb (500 g) leg of lamb, boned and cut into 1-inch (2.5-cm) cubes

3 onions, quartered

6 red dates, pitted

1 piece dried mandarin peel, soaked in water for 1 hour, drained

5–6 slices fresh ginger

5–6 cloves garlic

1 star anise

1 tablespoon light soy sauce

1 tablespoon dark soy sauce

1 tablespoon Chinese rice wine

4 cups (32 fl oz/1 liter) water

salt

◈ Place the lamb in a large saucepan and add enough water to cover. Slowly bring to a boil and cook for 10 minutes. Remove from the heat and drain. Wash and dry the pan.

◈ Place the lamb and all of the remaining ingredients, except for the salt, in the clean saucepan. Bring to a boil, then reduce the heat, cover, and simmer for 1½ hours. Add salt to taste. Remove the mandarin peel and star anise, and serve immediately.

italian
mixed vegetable soup

serves 4

2 tablespoons extra virgin olive oil

3 small white onions, thinly sliced

3 oz (90 g) pancetta, diced

5 oz (155 g) ground (minced) lean young beef (yearling beef)

3 tablespoons shelled green peas

6 artichoke hearts, cut into wedges

30 asparagus tips

3 tablespoons shelled fava (broad) beans

4 cups (32 fl oz/1 liter) beef stock, boiling

coarse country bread, cubed and toasted

❖ Heat the oil in a large saucepan over medium-high heat. Add the onions and cook, stirring often, until golden. Add the pancetta and beef and cook, stirring often, for 10 minutes, or until well browned.

❖ Stir in the peas, artichokes, asparagus, fava beans, and boiling stock. Cook for 15 minutes. Serve immediately, topped with the toasted cubes of bread.

superior broth

makes 10 cups (2½ qt/2.5 l)

Superior broth is the soul of great Chinese cooking, comparable in aroma, depth, and complexity to a vintage wine. Because Chinese chefs never throw anything away, any leftovers from making Superior Broth can be used to make Secondary Broth (recipe opposite), which is more than adequate for most everyday recipes.

2½ lb (1.25 kg) chicken pieces

2½ lb (1.25 kg) lean pork, cut into large pieces

2 lb (1 kg) Chinese or Virginia ham, cut into large pieces

15 cups (3¾ qt/3.75 l) water

4 oz (125 g) ginger, lightly crushed

6 green (spring) onions, trimmed

3 pieces dried orange peel

❖ Place the chicken, pork, and ham in a large saucepan. Add enough water to cover the meats. Slowly bring to a boil, then cook for 10 minutes. Drain and rinse the meats.

❖ Bring the 15 cups (3¾ qt/3.75 l) water to a boil in a very large saucepan or stockpot. Add the meats and all of the remaining ingredients. When the mixture returns to a boil, reduce the heat and simmer, uncovered, for 5 hours. Remove from the heat and strain through a fine-mesh sieve lined with cheesecloth (muslin) into a clean container. Discard the solid ingredients or use to make Secondary Broth (recipe at right).

❖ Both of these broths can be used immediately, or cooled, covered, and refrigerated for up to 5 days or frozen for up to 1 month. Before using or freezing, lift off and discard the fat congealed on the surface.

secondary broth

Reserve all of the solid ingredients used to make the Superior Broth and place in a large saucepan. Add 12 cups (3 qt/3 l) water and bring to a boil. Reduce the heat and simmer, uncovered, for 2½ hours. Strain the liquid as before and discard the solid ingredients.

makes 10 cups (2½ qt/2.5 l)

pork ribs, octopus, and cabbage soup

serves 6–8

2 lb (1 kg) pork spare-ribs

12 cups (3 qt/3 l) water

2 oz (60 g) fresh ginger, finely chopped

⅓ piece dried mandarin peel, soaked in water for 30 minutes, drained

1 dried octopus (3–4 oz/ 90–125 g), soaked in water for 1–2 hours, drained and chopped

1½ lb (750 g) green cabbage, chopped

3 dried figs, chopped

Place the spare-ribs in a large saucepan and add enough water to cover. Bring to a boil and cook for 5 minutes. Drain the meat and rinse well. Wash and dry the saucepan.

Place the 12 cups (3 qt/3 l) water, the ginger, and mandarin peel in the clean pan and bring to a boil. Add the meat and all of the remaining ingredients. When the water returns to a boil, reduce the heat and simmer for 3 hours. Remove the mandarin peel and serve immediately.

oxtail soup

serves 6

1 oxtail, cut into bite-sized pieces
and trimmed of excess fat

8 oz (250 g) beef shin (shank),
cut into bite-sized pieces

8 cups (64 fl oz/2 l) water

2 pieces dried mandarin peel

small knob of fresh ginger

salt

1 small (6 oz/185 g) Chinese turnip
(lor buk), diagonally sliced

1 medium carrot (6 oz/185 g),
peeled, diagonally sliced

1 white onion, quartered

chopped green (spring) onion,
for garnishing

❖ Plunge the oxtail pieces into a saucepan
of boiling water to clear the meat of any
impurities and excess fat. Refresh under
cold running water.

❖ Place the oxtail and beef shin in a
stockpot with the 8 cups (64 fl oz/2 l)
water. Add the mandarin peel, ginger, and
salt and simmer for 1 hour.

❖ Stir in the Chinese turnip, carrot, and
onion. Simmer gently for 30 minutes more.

❖ Remove the mandarin peel and serve
immediately, sprinkled with green onion.

green soup
with kale and potatoes

serves 4

¼ cup (2 fl oz/60 ml) olive oil

1 large yellow onion, chopped

2 cloves garlic, finely chopped

3 baking potatoes, about 1 lb (500 g) total weight, peeled and thinly sliced

6 cups (48 fl oz/1.5 l) water

salt and ground black pepper

12 oz (375 g) kale, washed

4 oz (125 g) chouriço, linguiça, or chorizo sausage

4 teaspoons olive oil, extra

❖ Heat the oil in a large saucepan over medium heat. Add the onion and cook until tender, about 8 minutes. Add the garlic and potatoes and cook, stirring, for 3 minutes. Add the water and 2 teaspoons of salt. Cover and simmer until the potatoes are very soft, about 20 minutes.

❖ Meanwhile, remove the tough stems from the kale. Stack the leaves, roll, and cut crosswise into fine strips.

❖ Cook the sausage in a frying pan over medium heat until cooked through, about 10 minutes. Cool, then slice.

❖ Use a potato masher to mash the potatoes in the liquid in the pan. Return to low heat, add the sausage, and cook, stirring, for 5 minutes. Add the kale, stir well and simmer, uncovered, for 4 minutes. Season with salt and pepper. Drizzle each serving with 1 teaspoon olive oil, and serve.

pork and cucumber soup

serves 4–6

1 teaspoon sugar

¼ teaspoon sesame oil

2 teaspoons cornstarch (cornflour)

1 tablespoon water

6 oz (185 g) pork fillet, cut into
2- x 1-inch (5- x 2.5-cm) strips

3 cups (24 fl oz/750 ml) water, extra

4 cups (32 fl oz/1 liter) Secondary Broth
(pages 158–159)

6 slices fresh ginger

½ teaspoon sesame oil, extra

1 teaspoon aromatic or cider vinegar

1 teaspoon salt

1 teaspoon Chinese rice wine

½ teaspoon ground black pepper

1 cucumber, seeded and cut into slivers

◈ Combine the sugar, ¼ teaspoon sesame oil, cornstarch, and 1 tablespoon water in a bowl. Add the pork, toss to coat, and set aside for 15 minutes to marinate.

◈ Bring the 3 cups (24 fl oz/750 ml) water to a boil in a large saucepan and add the pork. When the water returns to a boil, drain the pork and set aside. Wash and dry the saucepan.

◈ Place the broth and ginger in the clean saucepan and bring to a boil. Stir in the ½ teaspoon sesame oil, vinegar, salt, rice wine, and pepper. Add the pork and cucumber and heat through. Serve.

sour and peppery soup

serves 4–6

2 teaspoons salt

1 teaspoon sugar

1 tablespoon cornstarch (cornflour)

2 tablespoons water

2 oz (60 g) pork fillet, cut into slivers

2 oz (60 g) uncooked shrimp (green prawns), peeled and deveined

2 cups (16 fl oz/500 ml) water, extra

4 cups (32 fl oz/1 liter) Secondary Broth (pages 158–159)

12 pieces cloud ear fungus, soaked in cold water for 30 minutes, drained

2 oz (60 g) bean curd, shredded

2 oz (60 g) bamboo shoots, sliced

1 tablespoon shredded fresh ginger

1 tablespoon chopped green (spring) onion

2 tablespoons aromatic or cider vinegar

1 teaspoon chile oil

½ teaspoon ground black pepper

1 teaspoon sugar

2 tablespoons cornstarch (cornflour), extra, dissolved in 2 tablespoons water

1 egg, beaten lightly

1 teaspoon Chinese rice wine

2 teaspoons dark soy sauce

Combine salt, sugar, cornstarch, and 2 tablespoons water in a bowl. Transfer half of the mixture to a separate bowl. Add the pork to one of the bowls and the shrimp to the other; toss well. Set aside to marinate for 15 minutes.

Bring the 2 cups (16 fl oz/500 ml) water to a boil in a large saucepan. Add the drained pork and cook for 1 minute. Add the drained shrimp and cook for 1 minute more. Discard the marinade. Drain the shrimp and pork and set aside. Wash and dry the pan.

Add the broth to the clean pan and bring to a boil. Stir in the fungus, bean curd, bamboo shoots, ginger, green onion, vinegar, chile oil, pepper, and sugar.

When the mixture returns to a boil, add the pork and shrimp. Stir in the dissolved cornstarch mixture, then stir in the egg. Add the rice wine and soy sauce and heat through before serving.

food fact

Cloud ear fungus is also known as "wood ear," "tree ear," or "black" fungus. This type of mushroom is black or dark-brown and comes in irregular frilled shapes. It has a delicate flavor and unusual, crunchy texture.

meatball soup
with cilantro pesto

serves 6–8

¾ cup (5½ oz/170 g)
short-grain white rice

1½ cups (12 fl oz/375 ml) boiling water

¼ cup (2 fl oz/60 ml) vegetable oil

2 white onions, diced

8 oz (250 g) ground (minced) pork

8 oz (250 g) ground (minced) beef

1 egg

1 teaspoon ground cumin

1 teaspoon dried oregano

1½ teaspoons salt

1 teaspoon ground black pepper

1 clove garlic, finely chopped

1 zucchini (courgette), diced

2 carrots, peeled and diced

2 ripe tomatoes, peeled, seeded, and diced

6 cups (48 fl oz/1.5 l) chicken stock

CILANTRO PESTO

½ cup (¾ oz/20 g) coarsely chopped
cilantro (fresh coriander)

1 sprig fresh mint, leaves chopped

juice of 2 limes

2 tablespoons olive oil

2 tablespoons water

½ teaspoon salt

✧ Place the rice in a heatproof bowl. Pour the boiling water over the rice. Soak for 40 minutes, then drain and set aside.

✧ Meanwhile, heat 2 tablespoons of the vegetable oil in a small saucepan over medium heat. Add half of the onion and cook, stirring often, until soft, about 5 minutes. Set aside to cool.

✧ Combine the pork, beef, cooled onion, soaked rice, egg, cumin, oregano, ¾ teaspoon of the salt, and ½ teaspoon of the pepper in a bowl. Use your hands to mix well and shape into 1-inch (2.5-cm) meatballs.

✧ Heat the remaining 2 tablespoons vegetable oil in a large stockpot over medium heat. Add the remaining onion and cook, stirring often, until soft, about 5 minutes. Add the garlic, zucchini, carrots, and tomatoes and cook, stirring, until fragrant, about 5 minutes. Add the chicken stock, stir well, and bring to a boil. Carefully slip the meatballs into the pot, reduce the heat to low, and simmer, uncovered, until the meatballs are cooked through, about 45 minutes. Stir in the remaining ¾ teaspoon salt and ½ teaspoon pepper.

✧ Meanwhile, for the cilantro pesto, combine the cilantro, mint, lime juice, olive oil, water, and salt in a small food processor or blender. Process or blend until the mixture forms a paste.

✧ Serve the soup immediately, topped with a dollop of the cilantro pesto.

wonton soup

8 oz (250 g) pork fillet, ground (minced)

2 teaspoons salt

1 teaspoon sesame oil

1 teaspoon cornstarch (cornflour)

4 oz (125 g) bamboo shoots,
finely chopped

1 lb (500 g) Chinese cabbage,
washed, dried, and finely chopped

48 wonton wrappers

6 cups (48 fl oz/1.5 l) boiling water

1 cup (8 fl oz/250 ml) cold water

4 cups (32 fl oz/1 liter) chicken stock

1 teaspoon Chinese rice wine

1 tablespoon light soy sauce

½ teaspoon ground black pepper

❖ Place the pork, salt, sesame oil, and cornstarch in a bowl and stir to combine. Add the bamboo shoots and cabbage and stir until well combined.

❖ Spoon about 1½ teaspoons of the pork mixture into the center of a wrapper. Wrap up and squeeze lightly. Repeat with the remaining pork mixture and wrappers.

❖ Drop the wontons into a large saucepan containing the boiling water. Add the cold water. When the water returns to a boil and the wontons float to the surface, remove and drain. Place wontons in soup bowls.

❖ Bring the stock to a boil in a saucepan. Stir in the rice wine, soy sauce, and pepper. Pour over the wontons and serve at once.

cantonese beef soup

1 teaspoon salt

1 teaspoon sugar

2 teaspoons cornstarch (cornflour)

1 tablespoon water

4 oz (125 g) ground (minced) beef fillet

2 cups (16 fl oz/500 ml) water, extra

4 cups (32 fl oz/1 liter) Secondary Broth (pages 158–159)

1 tablespoon shredded fresh ginger

1 tablespoon chopped green (spring) onion

1 tablespoon light soy sauce

1/2 teaspoon ground black pepper

1 teaspoon sesame oil

1 teaspoon Chinese rice wine

2 tablespoons cornstarch (cornflour), extra, dissolved in 2 tablespoons water

2 egg whites

1 tablespoon chopped cilantro (fresh coriander)

❖ Combine the salt, sugar, cornstarch, and 1 tablespoon water in a bowl. Add the beef and set aside for 15 minutes.

❖ Bring the 2 cups (16 fl oz/500 ml) water to a boil in a saucepan. Stir in the beef. When the beef turns white, remove from the pan and drain.

❖ Bring the broth to a boil in a clean saucepan. Stir in the ginger, green onion, soy sauce, pepper, sesame oil, rice wine, and cornstarch mixture. Stir in the egg whites. Add the beef and cilantro, and heat through.

pork and hominy in red chile broth

serves 4–6

serves 4–6

Hominy is made by drying corn kernels on the cob and then removing and soaking them in a solution of baking soda, lime, or wood ash. The kernels are then hulled, the germ is removed, and they are dried. Hominy resembles popcorn but is softer in texture.

1 lb (500 g) boneless stewing pork, cut into 1-inch (2.5-cm) cubes

½ teaspoon salt

4 cups (32 fl oz/1 liter) water

4 dried ancho chiles, stemmed and deseeded

5 cloves garlic

1½ teaspoons dried oregano

2 tablespoons vegetable oil

1 large yellow onion, diced

2 cups (12 oz/375 g) well-drained canned hominy

3 cups (24 fl oz/750 ml) chicken stock, or as needed

sliced radishes, shredded lettuce, diced yellow onion, corn tortilla chips, diced avocado, and lime wedges, to serve

✤ Combine the pork, salt, and water in a saucepan over high heat. Bring to a boil, then reduce the heat to medium and simmer gently, uncovered, until the pork is barely tender, about 20 minutes. Remove from the heat and let the pork cool in the liquid. Drain the pork, reserving the liquid in a bowl. Cover the pork with a damp kitchen towel and set aside.

✤ Place the chiles in the reserved warm cooking liquid for 20 minutes to soak. Transfer the liquid and chiles to a blender. Add the garlic and oregano and blend until smooth. Set aside.

✤ Heat the vegetable oil in a large saucepan over medium-high heat. Add the onion and cook, stirring often, until light golden, about 10 minutes. Stir in the chile mixture, hominy, and chicken stock. (Add more stock if needed to achieve a soupy consistency.) Stir in the reserved pork. Bring to a boil, then reduce the heat to medium-low and simmer gently, uncovered, until the pork is tender, about 30 minutes. Taste and adjust the seasonings, if necessary.

✤ Place the radishes, lettuce, onion, tortilla chips, avocado, and lime wedges in separate small bowls. Ladle the soup into serving bowls and serve accompanied by the garnishes.

serves 6

⅓ cup (2½ fl oz/80 ml) extra virgin
olive oil

3 oz (90 g) pancetta, chopped

1 onion, chopped

1 carrot, chopped

1 celery stalk, chopped

1¼ lb (625 g) plum (Roma) tomatoes,
peeled and diced

3 oz (90 g) beef (rump
roast), cubed

1¼ lb (625 g) shelled fresh fava
(broad) beans

8 cups (2 qt/2 l) clear chicken stock

salt and ground pepper

❖ Heat the oil in a frying pan and cook
the pancetta, onion, carrot, and celery,
stirring often, until the onion is
translucent, about 5 minutes.

❖ Stir in the tomatoes, beef, and fava
beans. Add the stock and cook over
low heat, stirring occasionally, for
30 minutes. Season to taste with salt
and pepper and serve at once.

fava bean soup;
ham and cheese rye muffins (page 232)

fava bean soup

split pea soup with bacon

serves 4–6

2 tablespoons olive oil

1 yellow onion,
finely chopped

1 celery stalk, thinly sliced

2 carrots, thinly sliced

1 clove garlic, finely chopped

1¼ cups (9 oz/280 g) green
split peas, rinsed

6 slices thick-cut bacon

7 cups (56 fl oz/1.75 l) water

1 bay leaf

¾ teaspoon salt, or to taste

¼ teaspoon ground pepper,
or to taste

1 tablespoon finely chopped
fresh parsley

split pea soup with bacon;
buttermilk biscuits (page 229)

❖ Heat the oil in a large, heavy-based saucepan over medium heat. Add the onion and cook, stirring, until softened, 3–5 minutes. Stir in the celery and carrots and cook until the carrots are tender, 2–3 minutes. Add the garlic and cook, stirring, for a further 1 minute.

❖ Stir in the split peas, bacon, water, and bay leaf. Increase heat to high and bring to a simmer. Reduce heat to medium-low, partially cover, and cook until the peas are soft, about 1 hour, stirring often and occasionally skimming off the scum that rises to the surface.

❖ Remove the bacon and bay leaf. Discard bay leaf. Cut the bacon into small pieces; set aside.

❖ In a blender or food processor, purée the soup until smooth and creamy. Return the soup to the pan.

❖ Reheat the soup over medium heat, stirring occasionally, until very hot. Season to taste with salt and pepper, then stir in the reserved bacon. Serve immediately, sprinkled with parsley.

irish lamb stew

serves 6

3½ lb (1.75 kg) lamb (a mix of shoulder, neck, and breast), cut into 2-inch (5-cm) cubes

salt and ground pepper

1 tablespoon peanut (groundnut) oil

3 tablespoons butter

2 celery stalks, finely chopped

2 shallots, finely chopped

1 carrot, finely chopped

1 teaspoon superfine (caster) sugar

2 cloves garlic, halved

⅓ cup (2½ fl oz/80 ml) dry white wine

6½ oz (200 g) ripe tomatoes, peeled, seeded, and chopped

2¼ cups (18 fl oz/560 ml) chicken stock

18 round baby onions

1 can (13½ oz/425 g) great Northern (white haricot) beans, rinsed and drained

chopped parsley (optional)

❖ Season the lamb with salt and pepper. Heat oil and butter in a 6-qt (6-l) saucepan. Working in batches, add some of the meat pieces and cook until browned on all sides. Remove with a slotted spoon and set aside. Repeat with the remaining meat. Add the celery, shallots, carrot, sugar, and garlic and cook over low heat, stirring, for 5 minutes. Add the wine and stir until it evaporates. Stir in the tomatoes and chicken stock and cook for 1 hour.

❖ Peel the onions and remove the green stems; wash and dry. Add the onions to the lamb mixture. Stir well and cook for a further 30 minutes.

❖ Add the beans to the lamb mixture. Cook for 30 minutes, or until the vegetables are tender. Serve at once, garnished with the parsley, if desired.

pork stew
with green chiles

serves 6–8

1½ lb (750 g) fresh or drained, canned tomatillos

4 lb (2 kg) pork butt or shoulder, fat trimmed, cut into 2-inch (5-cm) cubes

2 teaspoons salt

1 teaspoon ground pepper

all-purpose (plain) flour, for dusting

¼ cup (2 fl oz/60 ml) vegetable oil

3 yellow onions, cut into 1-inch (2.5-cm) pieces

2 fresh green anaheim or poblano chiles, stemmed, seeded, and cut into 1-inch (2.5-cm) pieces

2 fresh green jalapeño chiles, stemmed, seeded, and finely chopped

2 green bell peppers (capsicums), seeded and cut into 1-inch (2.5-cm) pieces

3 cloves garlic, finely chopped

1 tablespoon dried oregano, crumbled

2 teaspoons ground cumin

2 tablespoons coriander seeds, crushed, soaked in water for 15 minutes, then drained

2 bay leaves

¼ cup (⅓ oz/10 g) coarsely chopped cilantro (fresh coriander)

4 cups (32 fl oz/1 liter) chicken stock

❖ If using fresh tomatillos, preheat a broiler (griller). Husk the tomatillos, then place in a baking pan and broil, turning occasionally, until charred. Cool, then core and chop. If using canned tomatillos, core and chop them.

❖ Season pork with salt and pepper, then dust with the flour. Heat the oil in a heavy-based frying pan over medium-high heat. Cook pork in batches until well browned. Place in a large soup pot.

❖ Discard fat in frying pan and return the pan to medium heat. Add onions and cook, stirring, until soft, about 5 minutes. Stir in chiles and bell peppers and cook until fragrant, 3–4 minutes. Add garlic and cook for 1–2 minutes.

❖ Add the onion mixture, tomatillos, oregano, cumin, coriander seeds, bay leaves, cilantro, and chicken stock to the soup pot. Bring to a boil, then reduce heat and simmer, uncovered, until the pork is very tender, 2–3 hours. Serve.

179

wonton
noodle soup

serves 6

NOODLES

8 oz (250 g) fresh Chinese egg noodles

1 tablespoon peanut oil

WONTONS

8 oz (250 g) uncooked shrimp (green
prawns), peeled and deveined

1½ teaspoons coarse (kosher) salt

¾ lb (375 g) medium-grind
(minced) pork butt

1 tablespoon Chinese rice wine
or dry sherry

2 teaspoons light soy sauce

1 green (spring) onion, finely chopped

2 tablespoons drained, finely chopped
canned bamboo shoots

¼ teaspoon sugar

large pinch white pepper

1 teaspoon sesame oil

1 teaspoon cornstarch (cornflour)

60 wonton wrappers

1 egg white, lightly beaten

SOUP

6 cups (48 fl oz/1.5 l) chicken stock

¼ teaspoon sugar

light soy sauce, to taste

1 tablespoon sesame oil

salt

1 lb (500 g) bok choy, cut into
2-inch (5-cm) lengths, or baby bok choy,
cut in half

1 green (spring) onion, chopped

❖ Gently pull strands of noodles apart. In a large saucepan of boiling salted water cook the noodles, stirring to separate strands, for 1 minute. Drain and rinse well. Drain again and place in a large bowl. Toss with the oil to prevent the strands sticking together.

❖ For the wontons, rinse the shrimp; drain. Place in a bowl with 1 teaspoon of the salt and toss well; set aside for 10 minutes. Rinse again, drain, and pat dry; chop coarsely. In a bowl, combine the shrimp, remaining ½ teaspoon salt, pork, wine or sherry, soy sauce, green onion, bamboo shoots, sugar, white pepper, sesame oil, and cornstarch.

❖ To wrap wontons, work with 1 wrapper at a time, keeping unused wrappers covered with a kitchen towel. Place 1 heaped teaspoon of filling in center of a wrapper. Moisten wrapper edges with water and fold in half to form a triangle. Bring the 2 long ends up and over to meet and slightly overlap. Brush overlapping edges with egg white and press to seal. Place on a baking sheet and cover with a kitchen towel. Repeat with remaining filling and wrappers. You will need 36 wontons for this dish; wrap the remainder and any unused wrappers in plastic wrap and freeze for up to 2 months.

❖ For the soup, heat the chicken stock in a saucepan. Season with sugar, soy sauce, and sesame oil. At the same time, cook the bok choy in a large saucepan of boiling lightly salted water for 1 minute. Use a slotted spoon to transfer to a bowl. When stock is hot, add noodles and reheat. Use the spoon to divide noodles among bowls; keep warm.

❖ Drop 36 wontons into boiling water. Cook until they float, about 3 minutes. Place wontons in bowls, add bok choy, and ladle over hot stock. Garnish with green onion.

minestrone
with barley

serves 4

1 cup (6 oz/185 g) pearl barley, soaked in cold water for 12 hours, drained

3 oz (90 g) sausage meat, crumbled

1 oz (30 g) prosciutto, finely chopped

1 celery stalk, diced

1 onion, diced

2–3 potatoes, peeled and diced

salt

14 cups (3½ qt/3.5 l) water

½ cup (2 oz/60 g) grated Parmesan cheese

❖ Cook the drained barley in boiling salted water for 45 minutes; drain.

❖ Meanwhile, plunge the sausage meat into boiling water and then squeeze it to remove the fat.

❖ In a large saucepan combine the sausage meat, prosciutto, celery, onion, potatoes, salt, and water. Simmer for 30 minutes. Stir in the barley and cook for 45 minutes more, or until it is soft and creamy. Place 2 tablespoons of cheese in each bowl and ladle the hot soup over the top. Serve immediately.

carrot muffins
with pesto

makes 10 muffins

1 cup (4 oz/125 g) all-purpose (plain) flour

¾ cup (3 oz/90 g) whole-grain (wholemeal) flour

1 tablespoon sugar

2 teaspoons baking powder

¼ teaspoon baking soda (bicarbonate of soda)

¼ teaspoon salt

1 egg, beaten lightly

¾ cup (6 fl oz/180 ml) milk

½ cup (1½ oz/45 g) finely shredded peeled carrot

¼ cup (2 fl oz/60 ml) cooking oil

4 tablespoons basil pesto (homemade, page 73, or purchased)

2 tablespoons grated Parmesan cheese

❖ Preheat an oven to 400°F (200°C/ Gas Mark 5). Grease ten 2½-inch (5–6-cm) muffin cups or line with paper baking cups.

❖ Combine flours, sugar, baking powder, baking soda, and salt in a bowl. Make a well in center. Combine egg, milk, carrot, and oil in a jug. Stir into dry mixture until just combined (the batter should be lumpy).

❖ Spoon 1 rounded tablespoon of batter into each muffin cup, top with 2 teaspoons of pesto, and then add the remaining batter, filling each cup two-thirds full. Sprinkle with the cheese. Bake for 20 minutes, or until golden. Turn onto wire racks to cool slightly. Serve with your favorite soup.

ham and cabbage soup

serves 4–6

2–3 tablespoons peanut oil

4 slices fresh ginger

1 lb (500 g) shredded
Chinese cabbage

4 cups (32 fl oz/1 liter)
Secondary Broth (page 159)

2 oz (60 g) Chinese or Virginia
ham, thinly sliced

❖ Heat the oil in a large wok or frying pan over high heat. Add the ginger and cabbage and cook, stirring constantly, for 2 minutes.

❖ Stir in the broth and bring to a boil. Reduce heat to medium, cover, and cook for 15 minutes. Add the ham and cook for 5 minutes more. Serve immediately.

moorish casserole

serves 4–6

1/3 cup (2 1/2 fl oz/80 ml) olive oil

12 raw almonds

1 thick slice French bread
(about 1 oz/30 g)

1 1/2 lb (750 g) beef and/or
liver, chopped

3 cloves garlic

4 black peppercorns

1 cinnamon stick

1 clove

pinch of cumin seeds

water as needed

1 teaspoon paprika

2 1/4 cups (18 fl oz/560 ml)
water

salt

❖ Heat the oil in a heatproof casserole over medium-high heat. Add the almonds and bread and cook, turning occasionally, until golden. Remove and set aside. Add the meat to the casserole and cook, stirring often, until browned.

❖ Meanwhile, use a mortar and pestle to crush the garlic, peppercorns, cinnamon, clove, and cumin seeds. Add the almonds and bread and crush until combined. Dilute the mixture with a small amount of water.

❖ Add the paprika to the casserole and stir well. Stir in the almond mixture, water, and a little salt.

❖ Cover and cook over low heat for about 1 hour, or until the beef or liver is very tender. Serve immediately.

spicy lamb soup

serves 8

This spicy Anglo-Indian hawker soup evolved from colonial India's mulligatawny soup. It is popular hawker fare in Malaysia and Singapore, where it is served with fried pappadums. Garnish with chopped celery leaves or cilantro (fresh coriander) leaves.

SPICE PASTE

1 piece fresh ginger, 1 inch (2.5 cm) long, peeled and coarsely chopped

6 cloves garlic

6 shallots, about 8 oz (250 g), halved

1½ teaspoons ground fennel

1½ teaspoons ground cumin

1 tablespoon ground coriander

3 tablespoons water, approximately

spicy lamb soup

SOUP

1½ lb (750 g) meaty lamb
bones for stock

12 cups (3 qt/3 l) water
or meat stock

2 tablespoons ghee or
vegetable oil

2 leeks, including 1 inch
(2.5 cm) of the tender green
tops, washed and sliced

1 teaspoon curry powder

2 cardamom pods, bruised

2 star anise

1 cinnamon stick

4 cloves

1 large carrot, peeled and
thickly sliced

2 teaspoons sugar

1½ teaspoons salt

1 large tomato,
cut into large wedges

fresh lime juice (optional)

❖ For the spice paste, place the ginger, garlic, shallots, fennel, cumin, and coriander in a blender. Blend to a smooth paste, adding the water as needed to facilitate blending. Set aside.

❖ For the soup, preheat an oven to 450°F (230°C/ Gas Mark 6). Remove any meat from the lamb bones, cut into 1-inch (2.5-cm) cubes, and set aside. Place the bones in a roasting pan and roast, turning occasionally, until browned, about 20 minutes. Transfer the bones to a plate and set aside.

❖ Drain off the fat from the roasting pan and place the pan over medium heat. When the pan is hot, add 2 cups (16 fl oz/500 ml) of the water or stock and deglaze the pan by stirring to dislodge any browned bits from the base of the pan. Set aside.

❖ Melt the ghee or heat the vegetable oil in a large stockpot over medium heat. Add the leeks and cook, stirring often, until golden, about 2 minutes. Add the

spicy lamb soup

spice paste and curry powder and stir until fragrant, about 1 minute. Add the roasted bones, reserved meat, the liquid from the roasting pan, and the remaining water or stock. Wrap the cardamom, star anise, cinnamon, and cloves in a piece of cheesecloth (muslin), tie securely with kitchen string, and add to the pot. Bring to a boil, then reduce the heat to low and simmer, uncovered, for 30 minutes. Stir in the carrot and simmer until the meat is tender, about 30 minutes. Season with sugar and salt, and stir in the tomato.

❖ Discard the cheesecloth bag and the bones and ladle the soup into serving bowls. Add lime juice to taste, if desired, and serve hot.

food fact

Pappadums are small dried lentil wafers that expand when cooked. To serve this soup with fried pappadums, heat a wok or saucepan over medium heat. Add peanut oil to a depth of 1 inch (2.5 cm) and heat until very hot. Add the pappadums, 1–2 at a time, and cook until puffed. Using tongs, turn and cook the other side. (They take only seconds to cook, so you need to move fast.) Drain on paper towels. They may be served hot, warm or cool. If you wish to seve them hot, keep them warm in a low oven while you fry the remaining pappadums.

hanoi
beef and noodle soup

serves 6

BEEF BROTH

3 lb (1.5 kg) oxtails, cut into sections

3 lb (1.5 kg) beef shins (shanks)

14 cups (3½ qt/3.5 l) water

3 pieces fresh ginger, each 1 inch
(2.5 cm) long, unpeeled

1 large yellow onion, unpeeled, cut in half

4 shallots, unpeeled

1 lb (500 g) Chinese radishes, cut into
2-inch (5-cm) chunks

3 carrots, unpeeled, cut into chunks

4 star anise

6 cloves

2 cinnamon sticks

¼ cup (2 fl oz/60 ml) fish sauce

salt

BEEF, NOODLES, AND ACCOMPANIMENTS

8 oz (250 g) beef round (1 piece,
at least 2 inches/5 cm thick)

1 lb (500 g) dried flat rice stick noodles,
¼-inch (6-mm) wide

1 large yellow onion

2 green (spring) onions

2 small fresh red chiles

1 cup (1 oz/30 g) cilantro
(fresh coriander) leaves

½ cup (½ oz/15 g) fresh mint leaves

1 lime, cut into 6 wedges

❖ For the broth, place the oxtails, beef shins, and water in a large stockpot and bring to a boil. Meanwhile, preheat a broiler (grill). Place the ginger, onion, and shallots on a baking sheet and broil, turning often, until browned on all sides, 1–2 minutes. Set aside.

❖ When the water is boiling, use a large spoon or wire skimmer to skim the scum from the surface until it is clear of foam, about 10 minutes. Stir in the browned vegetables and the radishes, carrots, star anise, cloves, and cinnamon sticks. Reduce the heat to medium-low, partially cover, and simmer gently for 3½ hours to concentrate the flavors.

❖ Remove from the heat and allow to cool. Strain the broth through a fine-mesh sieve into a bowl; discard the solids. Set aside until the fat rises to the surface. Use a large spoon to skim off and discard the fat. Stir in the fish sauce and salt to taste. You should have about 8 cups (64 fl oz/2 l) broth. (The broth can be made 1 day in advance and refrigerated, covered.)

❖ For the beef, wrap in plastic wrap and freeze until partially frozen, about 1 hour.

❖ Meanwhile, for the noodles, place in a large bowl, add enough warm water to cover, and set aside until the noodles are soft and pliable, about 20 minutes. Drain and set aside.

❖ Cut the beef across the grain into paper-thin slices about 3 inches (7.5 cm) long. Set aside.

❖ Place the broth in a large saucepan and bring to a boil. Reduce the heat to keep the broth at a gentle simmer. Thinly slice the yellow and green onions and the chiles; set aside.

hanoi beef and noodle soup

❖ Bring a medium saucepan of water to a boil. Add the noodles and boil until tender, about 1 minute. Drain well and then divide the noodles evenly among 6 deep soup bowls.

❖ Divide the onions, slices of beef, and chiles evenly among the soup bowls. Ladle the hot broth over the top (it will cook the beef). Garnish with the cilantro and mint. Serve with lime wedges.

cantonese
steamboat

serves 6–8

This recipe is an adaptation of the Mongolian hotpot, in which thinly sliced meat and leafy vegetables are dropped into boiling chicken broth (kept hot in a special pot called a steamboat) to cook. The meat and vegetables are lifted out and eaten with a selection of dipping sauces. Noodles are then added to the broth to make a flavorsome soup.

SOUP

12 cups (3 qt/3 l) chicken stock

4 slices fresh ginger

2 green (spring) onions, cut into 1½-inch (4-cm) lengths

salt and ground black pepper, to taste

MEATS

6 oz (185 g) lean chicken breast fillet, thinly sliced

6 oz (185 g) lean pork fillet, thinly sliced

6 oz (185 g) lean beef fillet, thinly sliced

6 oz (185 g) uncooked shrimp (green prawns) or mussels, clams, oysters, or scallops, cleaned as necessary

6 oz (185 g) lean white fish fillets, thinly sliced

cantonese steamboat

VEGETABLES

*green leafy vegetables, such as Chinese cabbage,
Tianjin cabbage (wong buk), hearts of cabbage
(choi sum), spinach (English spinach), or lettuce,
washed, tough parts of stalks removed,
and cut into 4-inch (10-cm) lengths*

*8 oz (250 g) fresh white mushrooms
(champignons), sliced*

*1 bunch green (spring) onions, trimmed and
cut into 2-inch (5-cm) lengths*

*4 oz (125 g) cellophane noodles (fun si), soaked
for 20 minutes in warm water, then cut into
6-inch (15-cm) lengths*

◈ For the soup, place the stock, ginger, and green onions in a large saucepan and bring to a boil over medium-high heat. Reduce heat and simmer, covered, for 10 minutes to blend the flavors. Taste and season with salt and pepper.

◈ Transfer the soup to a steamboat, hotpot, or electric frying pan and place in the center of the table. It is best to serve the meal at a round table so that all the diners can reach the boiling soup.

◈ Place the chicken, pork, beef, seafood, fish, leafy vegetables, mushrooms, green onions, and noodles in separate

cantonese steamboat

dishes and arrange them around the soup. Place the dipping sauces (see recipes, right) in small bowls and arrange them on the table.

❖ The diners select raw foods and cook them by placing them in the boiling soup for just a few seconds. Miniature wire baskets or chopsticks are used to remove the foods, which are then eaten with the preferred dipping sauce.

❖ The soup should be kept at a rolling boil. It is also best to cook the meats and seafood before the vegetables and noodles as they take longer to cook and will flavor the soup.

dipping sauces

These simple-to-make dipping sauces give wonderful flavor to the cooked meats, seafood, fish, vegetables, and noodles in the steamboat.

ginger soy Combine ½ cup (4 fl oz/125 ml) light soy sauce with 2 teaspoons finely chopped fresh ginger and a few drops of sesame oil.

chinese mustard Stir ¼ cup (2 fl oz/60 ml) boiling water into ¼ cup (2 oz/60 g) dry English or French mustard. Add 2 teaspoons peanut oil, ½ teaspoon salt, and 2–3 drops of vinegar.

hoisin sauce Combine 1 teaspoon hoisin sauce (available at Chinese stores), 1 tablespoon tomato ketchup, ¼ teaspoon vinegar, ½ teaspoon sugar, and ½ teaspoon soy sauce.

peanut Combine ½ cup (4 oz/125 g) smooth peanut butter, 1½ teaspoons dark soy sauce, 1 tablespoon water, ½ teaspoon finely chopped garlic, and 1 teaspoon tomato ketchup.

spanish meat and chickpea stew

serves 6

12 cups (3 qt/3 l) cold water

1 lb (500 g) beef shin (shank)

½ chicken, boned
(approximately 13 oz/410g)

3½ oz (105 g) pork fat (optional)

3½ oz (105 g) cured ham

1 lb (500 g) chickpeas (garbanzo beans),
soaked overnight, drained

1 salted pig's foot (trotter),
soaked overnight, drained

½ small onion (4 oz/125 g),
stuck with a clove

salt

8 oz (250 g) green beans, trimmed

8 oz (250 g) green cabbage, chopped

6½ oz (200 g) large white stalks of Swiss
chard (silverbeet), cleaned and chopped

9½ oz (295 g) Swiss chard
(silverbeet), washed

6½ oz (200 g) chorizo sausage

6 small potatoes (1¼ lb/625 g total
weight), peeled

few strands of saffron

2 morcilla blood sausages
(black puddings) (6½ oz/200 g total weight)

2½ oz (75 g) vermicelli

¼ cup (2 fl oz/60 ml) olive oil

1 clove garlic, peeled

tomato ketchup, to serve (optional)

❖ Place the water in a large stockpot over medium-high heat. When the water begins to simmer, add the beef shin, chicken, pork fat, if using, and ham. There should be enough water to cover all of these ingredients. Use a slotted spoon to skim any scum from the surface. When the water comes to a boil, add the chickpeas and pig's foot and return to a boil. Add the onion and salt, reduce the heat, and simmer gently for 3 hours.

❖ Place the beans, cabbage, chard stalks, chard, and chorizo in a large saucepan and cook over medium heat, stirring occasionally, for 30 minutes. Add the potatoes and saffron and cook, stirring occasionally, for 20 minutes more. Bring a medium saucepan of water to a boil and boil the blood sausages, taking care to keep them whole, until just cooked; drain.

❖ Strain the liquid from the stockpot and the vegetable mixture into a separate large saucepan over medium heat. Adjust the seasoning, if necessary, and add the vermicelli.

❖ Heat the oil in a frying pan and add the garlic and cooked green vegetables. Cook, stirring often, for 2 minutes, or until lightly browned. Transfer to a serving dish. Slice the chorizo and blood sausages and arrange next to the vegetables. Add the whole potatoes to the serving dish.

❖ Place the chickpeas on a large serving dish. Cut the beef into small chunks and place on top. Chop the chicken, pork fat, if using, ham, and pig's foot and arrange around the edge of the dish.

❖ The vermicelli soup and meat and vegetable dishes should all be served at the same time, accompanied, if desired, by tomato ketchup.

sour hot soup

serves 6–8

2 tablespoons white vinegar

2 tablespoons light soy sauce

2 tablespoons chopped green
(spring) onions

1 teaspoon sesame oil

1 teaspoon Sichuan peppercorns
(fagara, available at Chinese stores),
ground to a powder

1 teaspoon chopped fresh or dried chiles
or ½ teaspoon chile sauce (available at
Chinese stores)

1 tablespoon finely chopped fresh ginger

1 tablespoon cilantro (fresh coriander),
cut into short lengths

1 teaspoon light soy sauce, extra

½ teaspoon sesame oil, extra

1 teaspoon cornstarch (cornflour)

8 oz (250 g) pork shoulder, thinly sliced

3 tablespoons peanut oil

8 cups (64 fl oz/2 l) water

1 teaspoon sugar

1 teaspoon salt

1 cup (4 oz/125 g) bamboo shoots,
cut into julienne strips

1 tablespoon cloud ear fungus, soaked
for 30 minutes, drained

3 tablespoons cornstarch (cornflour),
extra, combined with enough cold
water to make a paste

3 fresh bean curd cakes, cut into
½-inch (13-mm) julienne strips

2 eggs, lightly beaten

◈ Place the vinegar, 2 tablespoons soy sauce, green onions, 1 teaspoon sesame oil, ground peppercorns, chiles, ginger, and cilantro in a soup tureen.

◈ Combine the 1 teaspoon soy sauce, ½ teaspoon sesame oil, and cornstarch in a medium nonaluminum dish. Add the pork and toss to coat. Set aside for 20 minutes to marinate.

◈ Heat the oil in a stockpot over medium heat. Add the pork and stir-fry until it changes colour. Transfer the pork to a plate.

◈ Add the water, sugar, and salt to the stockpot and bring to a boil. Stir in the bamboo shoots, cloud ear fungus, and cooked pork. Simmer for 5 minutes.

◈ Stir in the cornstarch paste and bring the soup to a boil. When the soup has a velvety consistency, stir in the bean curd. Gently stir in the beaten eggs until they float in soft tendrils. Add the soup to the soup tureen and serve immediately.

pork and cellophane noodle soup

serves 6–8

2 tablespoons peanut oil

2 slices fresh ginger (¼ inch/4 mm thick)

4 oz (125 g) pork fillet, shredded into
2-inch (5-cm) lengths

2 teaspoons Chinese rice wine or dry sherry

6 cups (48 fl oz/1.5 l) Family Chicken Broth
(page 246)

6 dried shiitake mushrooms, soaked for
45 minutes, drained, stalks discarded,
thinly sliced

2 oz (60 g) carrot, peeled,
cut into julienne strips

4 oz (125 g) zucchini (courgette),
cut into julienne strips

1½ tablespoons preserved mustard greens
(mui choi) or Sichuan preserved vegetables
(jar choi) (available at Chinese stores),
shredded, optional

1 oz (30 g) cellophane noodles (fun si),
soaked for 30 minutes in warm water,
drained, cut into 6-inch (15-cm) lengths

½ teaspoon salt

pinch of ground white pepper

¼ teaspoon sugar

½ teaspoon sesame oil

❖ Heat the peanut oil in a stockpot over high heat until it is just beginning to smoke. Add the ginger and stir-fry until fragrant. Add the pork and stir-fry until it changes color. Stir in the rice wine. Add the broth, mushrooms, and carrot and simmer for 10 minutes.

❖ Stir in the zucchini, preserved mustard greens (if using), and noodles and simmer for 2 minutes. Stir in the salt, pepper, sugar, and sesame oil and serve immediately.

recipe variations

You can replace the dried shiitake mushrooms with other dried mushrooms, dried cloud ear fungus, or any variety of fresh mushrooms, if desired. If using fresh mushrooms, there is no need to soak them.

spanish
red bean soup

serves 4

Beans occupy a privileged position in Spanish cuisine and feature in many dishes. There are many varieties, shapes, and colors of bean and each region has its favorites. This recipe is from Basque Country in northern Spain, where red kidney beans are much loved.

1 lb (500 g) red kidney beans, soaked overnight, drained

1½ onions (finely chop the whole onion; leave the half onion in one piece)

½ cup (4 fl oz/125 ml) olive oil

3½ oz (105 g) pork fat (optional)

8 oz (250 g) pork spare-ribs

salt

½ green cabbage, shredded

2 blood sausages (black puddings), 3½ oz (100 g) each

2 cloves garlic, crushed

❖ Place the beans in a large saucepan and cover with cold water. Stir in the onion half, 2 tablespoons of the oil, and the pork fat, if using. Cook over low heat, adding more cold water as the beans cook and the broth reduces. When the beans are half-cooked, after about 1¼ hours, stir in the spare-ribs and salt to taste. Cook until the beans are soft and a thick broth has formed, about 1 hour more. Remove the half onion.

❖ Heat ¼ cup (2 fl oz/60 ml) of the remaining oil in a large frying pan. Add the chopped onion and cook, stirring often, until it begins to brown. Stir in the bean mixture and cook over low heat for 40 minutes.

❖ Boil the cabbage in a separate saucepan for 15 minutes, until it is half-cooked. Add the blood sausages and season with salt to taste. Cook for 15 minutes more, then drain well, slice, and transfer to a serving dish.

❖ Heat the remaining oil in a small frying pan. Add the garlic and cook, stirring, until fragrant. Sprinkle over the cabbage.

❖ Serve the bean soup piping hot, accompanied by the cabbage and sausages.

lamb and red bell pepper stew

serves 4

Tender chunks of lamb with garlic and sweet red bell pepper make this easy stew a one-dish meal. Serve it with coarse country bread to mop up the delicious juices.

5 cloves garlic, peeled (4 minced and 1 whole)

2 lb (1 kg) lamb shoulder, cut into even-sized chunks

1/3 cup (2 1/2 fl oz/80 ml) olive oil

3 1/2 oz (105 g) cured ham, chopped

8 oz (250 g) carrots, peeled and sliced

2 tomatoes (8 oz/250 g total weight), peeled and finely chopped

1 red bell pepper (capsicum), chopped

1 sprig fresh parsley

1/3 cup (2 1/2 fl oz/80 ml) dry white wine

salt

8 oz (250 g) fresh peas, shelled

✥ Rub the minced garlic into the lamb chunks and set aside for 30 minutes.

✥ Heat the oil over high heat in a large frying pan. Add the ham and cook, stirring, for 30 seconds, then transfer to a heatproof casserole. Add the lamb chunks to the frying pan and cook, turning often, until lightly browned. Place the lamb chunks in the casserole on top of the ham. Add the carrots, tomatoes, and bell pepper to the frying pan and cook, stirring often, until golden.

✥ Meanwhile, use a mortar and pestle to crush the whole clove of garlic and the parsley. Add the wine to dilute the mixture. Add to the frying pan and stir well to combine. Pour the bell pepper mixture into the casserole and season with salt. Cover and cook over high heat, shaking the casserole often to prevent sticking, for 20 minutes. Stir occasionally, taking care that the liquid on the inside of the lid falls back into the casserole. Stir in the peas and cook for a further 20 minutes. Serve immediately.

recipe variations

Canned chopped tomatoes may be used instead of fresh tomatoes, if desired. Fresh mushrooms, cut into chunks if large; chopped eggplant (aubergine); and/or chopped zucchini (courgette) can be added to the casserole with the peas, if you would like a heartier dish.

pork
in peanut sauce

The thin yet creamy sauce
in this Mexican recipe is a
specialty of Veracruz, where
peanuts are cultivated.
This dish works equally
well with chicken.

8 cups (64 fl oz/2 l) water

5 cloves garlic

½ onion

1 teaspoon salt, or to taste

2 lb (1 kg) lean pork rump

⅓ cup (2½ fl oz/80 ml) vegetable oil

2 potatoes

2 lb (1 kg) tomatoes

2 serrano chiles, or to taste

5 oz (155 g) raw peanuts, skinned

5 oz (155 g) sesame seeds

ground cloves, to taste

ground cinnamon, to taste

steamed white rice, to serve

❖ Bring the water to a boil in a large saucepan. Add 2 cloves of garlic, the half onion, the salt, and pork and simmer for 20 minutes. Strain the liquid through a fine-mesh sieve into a large bowl. Cut the pork into 1¼-inch (3-cm) cubes. Reserve the garlic and onion. Reserve the cooking liquid separately.

❖ Heat 4 tablespoons of the oil in a large frying pan over medium heat. Add the pork and cook for 15 minutes, until cooked through and well browned. Drain on paper towels. Set aside.

❖ Boil the potatoes until they are cooked but still firm. Peel and then cut the potatoes into 1¼-inch (3-cm) cubes. Set aside.

❖ Roast the tomatoes and the remaining garlic on a hot cast-iron griddle or under a hot broiler (grill). Set aside. Roast the chiles until they turn darker and are fragrant, then the peanuts until lightly browned, and then the sesame seeds until golden. (Be careful not to burn the seeds or they will become bitter.) Coarsely process the roasted ingredients in a food processor with ½ cup (4 fl oz/125 ml) of the reserved cooking liquid. Add the reserved cooked garlic and onion, clove, and cinnamon. Process to combine.

❖ Heat the remaining 2 tablespoons of oil in a large saucepan over medium heat. Add the peanut mixture and cook, stirring often, for 5 minutes. Reduce the heat to low and simmer for 20 minutes. Stir in the pork, potatoes, and enough of the reserved cooking liquid to thin the sauce. Simmer for 10 minutes. The consistency should be that of a light sauce (quite liquid).

❖ To serve, spoon the pork mixture around the outside edge of a large serving plate and fill the center with the steamed rice.

pot-au-feu

serves 10

This hotpot is a classic
French boiled dinner,
prepared in a quantity large
enough for a big family-style
meal. This slow-cooking,
one-pot recipe provides both
a first and second course,
making it an excellent choice
for casual entertaining.

1 beef chuck roast or beef brisket, 3½ lb (1.75 kg)

1 lb (500 g) beef marrow bones

1 yellow onion, studded with 2 cloves

1 roasting chicken, about 4 lb (2 kg), trussed

4 celery stalks

3 leeks, trimmed, halved lengthways, and well rinsed

3 carrots, peeled and cut into 3-inch (7.5-cm) lengths

2 parsnips, peeled and cut into 3-inch (7.5-cm) lengths

1 turnip, peeled, quartered

1 tablespoon salt

1 teaspoon dried thyme

2 bay leaves

6 fresh flat-leaf (Italian) parsley sprigs

8 peppercorns

10 slices French bread

Cornichons (French-style pickles) or gherkins,
to serve (optional)

Dijon mustard, to serve

✤ Place the beef and the marrow bones in a large stockpot. Add enough water to cover and bring to a boil over medium-high heat. Boil for 5 minutes, using a slotted spoon to skim any scum that rises to the surface. Reduce the heat to medium-low, add the onion, and simmer, uncovered, for 3 hours.

✤ Add the chicken to the stockpot. Add more water if needed to cover the chicken and return to a boil. Boil for 5 minutes, using a slotted spoon to skim any scum that rises to the surface. Reduce the heat to low and add the celery, leeks, carrots, parsnips, turnip, salt, thyme, bay leaves, parsley, and peppercorns. Stir to combine. Simmer, uncovered, until the chicken juices run clear when it is pierced with a knife, and a knife can be inserted into the beef without resistance, about 1½ hours.

✤ After about 1 hour 10 minutes of simmering, preheat an oven to 300°F (150°C/Gas Mark 2). Place the bread slices on a baking sheet and cook in the oven, turning once, until they are crisp, about 10 minutes. Remove from the oven and set aside. Reduce the oven temperature to 175°F (80°C/Gas Mark ¼).

✤ Use a pair of tongs to transfer the chicken and beef to a large ovenproof platter. Use a slotted spoon to transfer the vegetables to the same platter. Cover loosely with aluminum foil and place in the oven. Line a large sieve with cheesecloth (muslin) and strain the broth through the sieve into a bowl. Discard the solids. Wipe out the stockpot and place the strained broth in it. Bring just to a boil and then remove from the heat.

pot-au-feu

❖ To serve, reserve enough of the hot broth to be used as a sauce for the meat and vegetables. Place in a small saucepan and warm through when ready to serve the second course. Place the slices of toast in shallow soup bowls. Ladle the remaining hot broth over the top and serve as a first course.

❖ For the second course, carve the beef thinly and then cut the chicken into small pieces. Serve with the vegetables, spooning a small amount of the warmed reserved broth over each portion. Accompany with the cornichons and mustard.

food fact

The tiny gherkins called cornichons may be served as an appetizer, or with cold meats, pâtés, and fish. Look for them in jars at delicatessens. If they are unavailable, small or sliced gherkins may be substituted.

beef
with green olives

serves 4–6

⅓ cup (2½ fl oz/80 ml) olive oil

1½ lb (750 g) beef, cut into small, thin steaks

1 small onion, finely chopped

1 green bell pepper (capsicum), chopped

2 tablespoons all-purpose (plain) flour

2¼ cups (18 fl oz/560 ml) water

¾ cup (6 fl oz/180 ml) rancio wine or any dry red wine

salt

6½ oz (200 g) green olives, pitted

◈ Heat the oil in a frying pan. Add the steaks and cook, turning once, until browned. Transfer to a heatproof casserole.

◈ Add the onion and bell pepper to the frying pan and cook, stirring often, until golden. Stir in the flour, then add to the casserole.

◈ Add the water, wine, and a little salt to the casserole, stir well and cook over low heat for 1 hour.

◈ Stir in the olives and cook for 30 minutes more. Serve immediately.

pork, asparagus, and baked egg casserole

serves 4

This simple Spanish dish celebrates local produce, including eggs and meat. The pork, ham, and sausage are covered in a creamy sauce, then the eggs and asparagus are placed on top and the mixture is baked just until the eggs set.

1/3 cup (2 1/2 fl oz/80 ml) olive oil

4 pork loin fillets (3 1/2 oz/105 g each)

salt

8 oz (250 g) longaniza (cured pork sausage), diced

2 oz (60 g) cured ham, diced

1 medium onion (5 oz/155 g), peeled and chopped

2 cloves garlic, finely chopped

1 bay leaf

1 teaspoon all-purpose (plain) flour

2/3 cup (5 fl oz/150 ml) dry white wine

2/3 cup (5 fl oz/150 ml) beef stock

4 eggs

4 cooked thick white asparagus spears
(fresh, canned, or frozen)

✧ Preheat an oven to 300°F (150°C/Gas Mark 2).

✧ Heat the oil in a frying pan over medium heat.
When hot, add the pork fillets and cook, turning once,
until well browned. Transfer to a medium casserole and
sprinkle with salt.

✧ Add the sausage and ham to the frying pan and
cook, stirring often, until lightly browned. Use a slotted
spoon to transfer to the casserole.

✧ Add the onion and garlic to the frying pan and
cook, stirring often, until they soften. Add the bay leaf.
Stir in the flour and cook until it browns, then stir in
the wine and stock to make a sauce that is smooth but
not too thick.

✧ Pour the sauce over the other ingredients in the
casserole. Carefully break the eggs on top, then
arrange the asparagus around them. Bake until the
eggs just set and serve immediately.

recipe variations

If longaniza is unavailable,
you can replace it with
chorizo sausage or another
similar spicy cured sausage.
Regular asparagus may be
substituted for the white
asparagus; if the spears are
thin, increase the amount.

cotechino and cabbage soup

serves 6

Cotechino are large, fresh pork sausages that are seasoned with nutmeg and cloves and salted for a few days. They are cooked in gently simmering water for 2–3 hours, then cut into thick slices and usually served on a bed of cabbage, mashed potatoes, lentils, or cooked dried beans.

1 cotechino sausage, about 1¾ lb (875 g)

1 cabbage, about 2 lb (1 kg)

1½ tablespoons butter

2 tablespoons extra virgin olive oil

1 onion, finely chopped

2 oz (60 g) pancetta, finely chopped

salt and ground black pepper

½ cup (4 fl oz/125 ml) dry white wine

1 cup (8 fl oz/250 ml) meat stock, boiling

3 tablespoons white vinegar

❖ Prick the sausage in several places with a needle or thin skewer. Wrap tightly in cheesecloth (muslin) and place in a saucepan of cold water. Bring slowly to a boil. Reduce the heat and simmer gently for about 2 hours. Set aside to cool in the cooking liquid. When cool, remove from the cheesecloth and slice.

❖ Separate the cabbage leaves, discarding the tough outer leaves and core. Wash the leaves thoroughly; drain well. Cut into thin strips.

❖ Heat the butter and oil in a saucepan over low heat. Add the onion and pancetta and cook, stirring often, for 5 minutes, or until softened. Add the cabbage and salt and pepper to taste and cook, stirring occasionally, until the cabbage wilts. Stir in the wine. Cover the pan, reduce the heat, and cook for 1¾ hours, adding some of the boiling stock as needed to keep the mixture moist.

❖ Sprinkle the cabbage mixture with the vinegar and add the slices of cotechino. Cover the pan and cook over low heat for 10 minutes. Serve immediately.

sausage and green bell pepper ragoût

serves 4

¼ cup (2 fl oz/60 ml) olive oil

1 lb (500 g) Greek loukanika or Italian sweet sausages, thickly sliced

1 lb (500 g) green bell peppers (capsicums), deseeded and cut lengthways into strips about 1 inch (2.5 cm) wide

1 lb (500 g) tomatoes, peeled, seeded, and chopped (fresh or canned)

1 tablespoon dried oregano

¼ teaspoon ground allspice (optional)

½ teaspoon ground coriander (optional)

2 teaspoons grated orange zest (rind) (optional)

salt and ground black pepper

❖ Heat 2 tablespoons of the olive oil in a large saucepan over high heat. Add the sausages and brown on all sides, about 5 minutes. Use a slotted spoon to transfer the sausages to a plate and set aside.

❖ Add the remaining 2 tablespoons of oil to the pan. Add the bell peppers and cook over medium heat until they soften.

❖ Add the sausages, tomatoes, and oregano to the pan; reduce heat to low. If using Italian sausages, add the allspice, coriander, and orange zest. Cover and simmer until sauce thickens, 15 minutes. Season with salt and pepper, and serve.

lamb stew
with artichokes

serves 4

3–4 tablespoons olive oil

2½ lb (1.25 kg) boneless lamb shoulder, trimmed of excess fat and cut into 2-inch (5-cm) pieces

3 onions, chopped

3 cloves garlic, finely chopped

1½ cups (12 fl oz/375 ml) water or chicken stock, or as needed

½ cup (4 fl oz/125 ml) fresh lemon juice

6 medium artichokes

2 lb (1 kg) assorted greens, such as romaine (cos) lettuce, dandelion greens, or Swiss chard (silverbeet), stems removed, rinsed, drained, and torn into bite-sized pieces (optional)

½ cup (¾ oz/20 g) chopped fresh dill

salt and ground black pepper

2 eggs, at room temperature

lamb stew with artichokes

◈ Heat 2 tablespoons of the olive oil in a large saucepan over high heat. Working in batches, add the lamb and brown on all sides, about 10 minutes. Use a slotted spoon to transfer the lamb to a large, heavy stockpot.

◈ Add more olive oil to the saucepan, if needed, and then add the onions. Cook over medium heat, stirring often, until softened, about 5 minutes. Add the garlic and cook for 3 minutes more. Transfer the onion mixture to the stockpot. Increase the heat to high, add ½ cup (4 fl oz/125 ml) of the water or stock to the saucepan, and deglaze the pan by stirring to dislodge any browned bits from the base. Add the pan juices to the stockpot.

◈ Add the remaining 1 cup (8 fl oz/ 250 ml) water or stock to the stockpot, or as needed to cover the meat. Bring to a boil, then reduce the heat to low, cover, and simmer for 45 minutes.

◈ Meanwhile, fill a large bowl three-quarters full with water and add ¼ cup (2 fl oz/60 ml) of the lemon juice. Snap off the tough outer leaves from the artichokes. Use a paring knife to trim the dark green parts from the base and stem. Cut the artichokes lengthwise into quarters, then scoop out and discard the prickly chokes. As they are cut, drop the artichokes into the bowl of lemon water to prevent discoloring. Set aside.

◈ If using the greens, bring a large saucepan of salted water to a boil. Add the greens and boil until tender, about 10 minutes; drain well.

lamb stew with artichokes

❖ When the lamb has been simmering for 45 minutes, drain the artichokes and add them to the stockpot along with the greens, if using. Simmer until the lamb and artichokes are tender, about 20 minutes more.

❖ Add the dill and season with salt and pepper to taste. Simmer for 5 minutes more. Beat the eggs in a bowl until they are very frothy. Gradually beat in the remaining ¼ cup (2 fl oz/60 ml) lemon juice. Gradually beat in about 1 cup (8 fl oz/250 ml) of the hot liquid from the stockpot, beating constantly to prevent the mixture from curdling. Slowly stir the egg mixture into the hot stew. Heat through but do not allow the stew to boil. Serve immediately.

recipe variations

While artichokes are the classic choice for this dill-scented stew, you could replace them with celery, fennel, or carrots. This stew (minus the egg mixture) can be prepared 1–2 days in advance; add the egg mixture during reheating.

flamenco eggs

serves 4

⅓ cup (2½ fl oz/80 ml) olive oil

1 onion (5 oz/155 g),
finely chopped

3½ oz (105 g) cured ham,
finely diced

1 lb (500 g) tomatoes, peeled
and finely chopped

3½ oz (105 g) peas, cooked

3½ oz (105 g) green
beans, cooked

5 oz (155 g) potatoes,
diced and fried until golden

3½ oz (105 g) chorizo sausage,
thinly sliced

salt and ground black pepper

4 eggs

❖ Preheat an oven to 350°F (180°C/Gas Mark 4).

❖ Heat the oil in a frying pan over low heat. Add the onion and cook, stirring often, until it begins to brown. Add the ham and cook, stirring often, for 2 minutes. Stir in the tomatoes. Cook until the mixture reduces a little, then add the peas, beans, and potatoes. Add the chorizo, season with salt and pepper to taste, and mix well. Cook until chorizo is cooked through, 2–4 minutes.

❖ Transfer to individual heatproof dishes and break an egg over the top of each. Bake until the eggs just set and serve immediately.

hearty
baked rice

serves 4

Throughout Spanish history, it has been common practice to cook rice in a heavy meat broth (stock). These baked rice dishes are traditionally prepared on Monday, to make use of the broth and any leftovers from Sunday's *cocido*, or mixed meat and vegetable stew (page 196). If you haven't made a *cocido*, don't worry, we've included substitutes in this recipe.

3 small tomatoes (10 oz/315 g)

¼ cup (2 fl oz/60 ml) olive oil

1 head garlic

1 medium potato (5 oz/155 g), sliced

2 onion-flavored blood sausages (black puddings) (8 oz/250 g total weight)

1 teaspoon paprika

1¾ cups (10 oz/315 g) medium-grain white rice

2¼ cups (18 fl oz/560 ml) cocido broth (page 196, omit the vermicelli) or meat stock, boiling

4 oz (125 g) chickpeas (garbanzo beans), cooked

6½ oz (200 g) cocido beef (or other cooked beef), boned and chopped

3½ oz (100 g) pork fat, chopped (optional)

salt

hearty baked rice

◈ Preheat an oven to 400°F (200°C/Gas Mark 6).

◈ Cut 2 of the tomatoes in half. Peel the remaining
tomato and finely chop. Heat the oil in a 14-inch
(35-cm) shallow, heatproof casserole. Add the whole
head of garlic and cook until browned. Stir in the
potato and cook until lightly browned. Add the halved
tomatoes, blood sausages, and the chopped tomato.
Add the paprika, followed immediately by the rice.
Stir quickly, then add the boiling broth. Stir in the
chickpeas, beef, and pork fat, if using. Distribute the
ingredients so the garlic is in the middle, surrounded by
the potato and halved tomatoes. Taste and adjust the
seasoning if necessary.

◈ When the mixture begins to bubble, transfer the
casserole to the oven and bake for 15–18 minutes,
or until the rice is tender. Serve immediately.

recipe hint

The blood sausage may be
replaced by any other type of
sausage, though the flavor of
the dish will vary accordingly.
Try using chorizo, Toulouse
sausage, or even regular or
flavored beef sausage.

braised pork
with quinces

serves 6

Quinces are prized in Greece and Turkey during the fall months, when their unique scent perfumes every kitchen. If you cannot find quinces, substitute apples or pears and reduce the sugar to 2 tablespoons. Although pork is a perfect partner for quince due to its natural sweetness, beef or lamb can also be used.

2½ lb (1.25 kg) boneless pork shoulder, trimmed of excess fat and cut into 2-inch (5-cm) cubes

2 teaspoons ground cinnamon

2 teaspoons ground cumin

1 lemon, juiced

3 lb (1.5 kg) quinces

2 tablespoons butter

½ cup (4 oz/125 g) sugar

1 cup (8 fl oz/250 ml) pomegranate juice or water

¼ cup (2 fl oz/60 ml) olive oil

2 onions, chopped

pinch of ground cayenne pepper (optional)

1 cup (8 fl oz/250 ml) chicken stock or water

salt and ground black pepper

braised pork with quinces

⬦ Rub the pork with 1 teaspoon each of the cinnamon and cumin. Place the spice-coated pork in a nonaluminum bowl, cover, and set aside at room temperature for 2 hours or place in the refrigerator overnight to marinate.

⬦ Fill a large bowl three-quarters full with water and add the lemon juice. Peel the quinces, core them, and then slice thickly. As they are cut, drop them into the bowl of lemon water to prevent discoloring.

⬦ Drain the quince slices and pat them dry with paper towels. Melt the butter in a saucepan over high heat. Add the quinces and cook, stirring often, until softened, about 10 minutes. Sprinkle with the sugar and continue to cook until golden, 15–20 minutes more. Add the pomegranate juice or water and simmer over medium heat until the quinces are tender, 15–20 minutes. Remove from the heat and set aside for 1 hour.

⬦ Return the quinces to a simmer over medium heat. Simmer for 15 minutes, then remove from the heat and set aside for 1 hour. Or, allow to cool, cover, and set aside overnight.

⬦ Heat the olive oil in a large, heavy saucepan over medium heat. Add the pork and brown on all sides, about 10 minutes. Using a slotted spoon, transfer the pork to a plate and set aside.

⬦ Add the onions to the saucepan and cook, stirring often, over medium heat until tender, about 8 minutes. Add the remaining cinnamon and cumin, and the cayenne pepper, if using.

braised pork with quinces

Cook, stirring often, for 2–3 minutes to blend the flavors and then return the pork to the pan. Add the 1 cup (8 fl oz/250 ml) chicken stock or water and stir to combine. Reduce the heat to low, cover, and simmer for 1 hour.

✥ Return the pan holding the quinces to medium heat and bring to a simmer. Simmer for 15 minutes. Add the quinces and their cooking liquid to the pork mixture and continue to simmer over low heat until the meat is tender and the flavors have blended, about 30 minutes. Season with salt and pepper. Serve immediately.

recipe hint

Quinces are irregular pear-shaped fruits with a downy skin and firm yellow flesh that has a bitter flavor when raw. When cooked, the color changes to deep pink and the bitterness softens. Due to their high pectin content, quinces are good for setting jams, jellies, and preserves.

pork meatballs
with cabbage

serves 4

1 tablespoon light soy sauce

1 teaspoon salt

1 teaspoon sugar

1 teaspoon sesame oil

2 teaspoons cornstarch (cornflour)

3 tablespoons water

6 oz (185 g) ground (minced) pork

1 cup (8 fl oz/250 ml) peanut oil

4–5 slices fresh ginger

2–3 cloves garlic

10 oz (315 g) cabbage, cut into
3-inch (7.5-cm) long strips

2 oz (60 g) fresh button mushrooms
(champignons), halved

2 cups (16 fl oz/500 ml) water

SAUCE

1 tablespoon light soy sauce

2 tablespoons oyster sauce

1 tablespoon Chinese rice wine

1 teaspoon salt

Combine the soy sauce, salt, sugar, sesame oil, cornstarch, and water in a bowl. Add the pork and stir with a fork until the mixture becomes sticky. Shape into balls 1 inch (2.5 cm) in diameter.

Heat the oil in a large wok or frying pan, add the meatballs, and cook until lightly browned all over. Remove from the wok; drain and set aside.

Drain all but 2–3 tablespoons of oil from the wok and reheat. Add the ginger and garlic and stir until fragrant. Add the cabbage and stir-fry for 1 minute. Add the mushrooms and stir-fry for 1 minute.

Add the water and meatballs to the wok. Cook over medium-low heat for 10 minutes.

Combine the sauce ingredients in a bowl. Add the sauce to the wok, stir to combine, and serve.

food fact

Chinese rice wine is a sweet, amber-colored wine that is made from fermented glutinous rice. It is used widely in Chinese cooking, especially in marinades and sauces, and can also be served warm and consumed with a meal. Dry sherry can be used if Chinese rice wine is unavailable.

rice
with pork and fava beans

serves 4

¼ cup (2 fl oz/60ml) olive oil

8 oz (250 g) lean pork, diced

13 oz (410 g) shelled fresh fava
(broad) beans

1 tomato (3½ oz/100 g),
peeled and finely chopped

1 teaspoon paprika

5⅔ cups (45 fl oz/1.4 l) chicken
or beef stock

pinch of saffron

salt

1⅓ cups (6½ oz/200 g)
medium-grain white rice

❖ Heat the oil in a casserole. Add the pork and cook, stirring often, until lightly browned. Add the fava beans and tomato and stir until combined. Stir in the paprika, followed immediately by the stock.

❖ Cook for 15–20 minutes, or until the fava beans are tender. Stir in the saffron.

❖ Taste and adjust the seasoning. Stir in the rice and cook, uncovered, over medium heat for 16–18 minutes, or until the rice is tender. Serve immediately.

buttermilk biscuits

2 cups (8 oz/250 g) all-purpose (plain) flour

2½ teaspoons baking powder

½ teaspoon salt

½ teaspoon baking soda (bicarbonate of soda)

½ cup (4 oz/125 g) chilled butter, chopped

¾ cup (6 fl oz/180 ml) buttermilk, chilled

❖ Combine the flour, baking powder, salt, and baking soda in a bowl. Add the butter and toss to coat. Using a pastry blender, 2 knives, or your fingertips, quickly cut or rub in the butter until the mixture is the consistency of coarse meal.

❖ Make a well in the center of the flour mixture. Add the buttermilk and stir with a fork until a soft dough forms that pulls away from the sides of the bowl.

❖ Preheat an oven to 450°F (220°C/Gas Mark 6).

❖ Turn the dough onto a lightly floured work surface. Knead very gently 5–6 times, until it just holds together. Gently pat or roll out the dough until ½-inch (13-mm) thick. Use a 2-inch (5-cm) round biscuit cutter to cut out rounds, pressing down and lifting the cutter without twisting. Place on an ungreased baking sheet, about 1½ inches (4 cm) apart. Gently knead the scraps together and cut another set of rounds.

❖ Bake for 10–12 minutes, or until evenly browned. Serve hot with soup or stew.

meatball stew

serves 4

SAUCE

¼ cup (2 fl oz/60 ml) olive oil

3½ oz (105 g) onion, finely chopped

1 carrot, peeled and thinly sliced

2 teaspoons all-purpose (plain) flour

3⅓ cups (27 fl oz/830 ml) beef stock

¼ cup (2 fl oz/60 ml) tomato purée

⅓ cup (2½ fl oz/80 ml) dry white wine

salt

MEATBALLS

3½ oz (105 g) bread, crusts removed

⅓ cup (2½ fl oz/80 ml) milk

8 oz (250 g) pork, ground (minced)

8 oz (250 g) beef, ground (minced)

1 tablespoon finely chopped fresh parsley

2 cloves garlic, finely chopped

salt

2 eggs

all-purpose (plain) flour, for coating

olive oil, for frying

❖ For the sauce, heat the oil in a heatproof casserole over low heat. Add the onion and carrot and cook, stirring often, for 10 minutes. Stir in the flour. When it begins to brown, add the stock, tomato purée, and wine. Add salt to taste and cook for 20 minutes.

❖ Meanwhile, for the meatballs, soak the bread in the milk, then squeeze out the excess milk. Combine the soaked bread, pork, beef, parsley, and garlic. Add salt to taste, then add the eggs and mix well. Lightly coat your hands with flour and shape the mixture into meatballs. Transfer the meatballs to a floured surface.

❖ Heat the oil in a frying pan. Add a few meatballs at a time and cook until browned all over. Transfer the meatballs to a heatproof casserole as they are cooked.

❖ Place the sauce in a blender and puree. Pour over the meatballs. Cook for 30 minutes over low heat. Serve immediately.

recipe variations

Serve this dish with slices of coarse country bread or buttermilk biscuits (page 229) to mop up the juices. Rice or mashed potato are also good accompaniments.

ham & cheese
rye muffins

makes 12 muffins

1¼ cups (5 oz/155g)
all-purpose (plain) flour

⅓ cup (1 oz/30 g) rye flour

2 teaspoons baking powder

2 teaspoons sugar

¼ teaspoon caraway seeds

¼ teaspoon onion salt

1 egg, beaten lightly

¾ cup (6 fl oz/180 ml) milk

¼ cup (2 fl oz/60 ml)
vegetable oil

⅔ cup (3 oz/90 g) finely
chopped cooked ham

1¼ cups (5 oz/155 g) shredded
Swiss or Gruyère cheese

❖ Preheat an oven to 400°F (200°C/Gas Mark 5).
Lightly grease twelve 2½-inch (5–6-cm) muffin cups
or line with paper baking cups.

❖ Combine the all-purpose flour, rye flour, baking
powder, sugar, caraway seeds, and onion salt in a
medium bowl. Make a well in the center.

❖ Combine the egg, milk, and oil in a jug. Add to the
dry ingredients with the ham and 1 cup of the cheese.
Stir until just combined. (The batter should be lumpy.)

❖ Spoon the mixture into the prepared muffin cups,
filling each two-thirds full. Bake for 20 minutes, or until
golden brown. Sprinkle with the remaining cheese.
Bake for 1 minute more, or until the cheese has melted.
Remove from pans and cool slightly on racks. Serve
warm, with your favorite soup or stew.

beef consommé
with cilantro

serves 6

8 cups (64 fl oz/2 l)
Supreme Chicken Broth
(page 248), strained

1 cup (8 fl oz/250 ml) sake
(Japanese rice wine)

1 lb (500 g) prime-quality beef
fillet (eye fillet), trimmed of
excess fat and sinew

salt and pepper to taste

1/2 bunch cilantro
(fresh coriander), washed,
dried, and cut into short
lengths, including stems

◈ Bring the broth to a boil in a stockpot. Stir in the sake, reduce the heat, and keep at a gentle simmer.

◈ Slice the beef fillet in half lengthwise and place on a cutting board with the cut-side down. Cut evenly on the diagonal into 1/4-inch (6-mm) thick slices.

◈ Add the beef to the broth and bring to a boil over medium heat. Reduce the heat to low and simmer for 1 minute. Taste and season with salt and pepper.

◈ Add the cilantro, stir gently to combine, and serve.

soups *with* poultry

classic chicken stock

makes 5 cups (40 fl oz/1.25 l) stock and 15 oz (425 g) meat

3¹⁄₂ lb (1.75 kg) bony chicken pieces (such as bones, necks, and wings from 3 chickens)

3 celery stalks with leaves, chopped

2 carrots, chopped

1 large onion, chopped

2 sprigs fresh parsley

1 teaspoon salt

¹⁄₂ teaspoon dried thyme, sage, or basil, crushed

¹⁄₄ teaspoon pepper

2 bay leaves

6 cups (48 fl oz/1.5 l) cold water

❖ Place chicken pieces, celery, carrots, onion, parsley, salt, thyme, sage, or basil, pepper, and bay leaves in a large stockpot. Add the water. Bring to a boil, then reduce the heat, cover and simmer for 2 hours. Remove the chicken pieces using a slotted spoon or tongs.

❖ Strain the stock through a large colander lined with 2 layers of cheesecloth (muslin) into a bowl. Discard the solids. If using while hot, skim fat. (Or, refrigerate for several hours or overnight, then lift off the layer of fat.)

❖ When the chicken is cool enough to handle, remove the meat from the bones and reserve meat for another use. Discard bones. Store the stock and reserved meat in separate airtight containers in the refrigerator for up to 3 days or in the freezer for up to 6 months.

spiced chicken stock

makes 6 cups (48 fl oz/1.5 l)

8 cups (2 qt/2 l) water

1 onion, studded with 2 cloves

4 cloves garlic, unpeeled

½ teaspoon black peppercorns

2 allspice berries

3 teaspoons salt, or to taste

2 lb (1 kg) chicken wings

◈ Place all the ingredients, except for the chicken, in a large stockpot and bring to a boil. Add the chicken and return to a boil. Use a slotted spoon to skim the scum from the surface. Reduce heat and simmer for 1 hour.

◈ Strain the stock through a large colander lined with 2 layers of cheesecloth (muslin) into a bowl. Discard the solids. Set aside to cool. Once cool, use a large or slotted spoon to lift off and discard the layer of fat that has formed on the surface.

◈ Store in an airtight container in the refrigerator for up to 3 days or in the freezer for up to 6 months.

chinese duckling
soup with pickled lime

serves 4–6

1 duckling, about 3 lb (1.5 kg)

4 cups (32 fl oz/1 liter) water

1 pickled lime

4 slices fresh ginger

1 tablespoon Chinese rice wine

4 cups (32 fl oz/1 liter)
Secondary Broth
(pages 158–159), boiling

❖ Chop the duckling into 6 pieces. Clean thoroughly and place in a large saucepan. Add the water and bring to a boil. Boil for 5 minutes, then remove the duck pieces and place on paper towels to drain.

❖ Place the duck pieces, lime, ginger, and rice wine in a large soup tureen with a lid. Add the broth and cover. Place the tureen on a steaming rack in a large stockpot of boiling water and steam for 3 hours. Serve.

chicken soup
with black mushrooms

serves 4–6

1 teaspoon salt

1 teaspoon sugar

1 teaspoon cornstarch (cornflour)

1 tablespoon water

2 teaspoons Chinese rice wine

4 oz (125 g) chicken breast, cut into
2- x 1-inch (5- x 2.5-cm) strips

2 cups (16 fl oz/500 ml) water, extra

4 dried shiitake mushrooms, soaked in
warm water for 1 hour, drained,
stems discarded

4 cups (32 fl oz/1 liter) Secondary Broth
(pages 158–159)

1 tablespoon shredded fresh ginger

1 tablespoon light soy sauce

¼ teaspoon sesame oil

Combine ½ teaspoon of the salt, ½ teaspoon of the sugar, the cornstarch, 1 tablespoon water, and 1 teaspoon of the rice wine in a bowl. Add the chicken, toss to coat, and set aside for 15 minutes to marinate.

Bring the 2 cups (16 fl oz/500 ml) water to a boil in a large saucepan and add the chicken. When the chicken becomes white, drain and set aside.

Cut the mushrooms into thin slivers. Combine the remaining salt, sugar, and rice wine in a heatproof bowl. Add the mushrooms and toss to coat. Place the bowl on a steaming rack in a saucepan of boiling water, cover the saucepan, and steam for 10 minutes. Remove from the saucepan and set aside.

Bring the broth to a boil in a large saucepan and add the ginger, chicken, and mushrooms. Stir in the soy sauce and sesame oil, and cook for 2 minutes. Serve immediately.

food fact

Cornstarch is also known as cornflour or maize flour. It is a very fine flour that is milled from the starch of corn kernels. Cornstarch is commonly used in Chinese cooking as a thickener, and is also used in baking.

noodle soup
with chicken and mushrooms

serves 4–6

1 teaspoon salt

1 teaspoon sugar

2 teaspoons Chinese rice wine

2 teaspoons cornstarch (cornflour)

1 tablespoon water

4 oz (125 g) chicken breast, cut into
2- x 1-inch (5- x 2.5-cm) strips

1 cup (8 oz/250 g) egg noodles

⅓ cup (2½ fl oz/80 ml) cold water

2 tablespoons peanut oil

1 tablespoon shredded fresh ginger

4 oz (125 g) cabbage, shredded

2 dried shiitake mushrooms, soaked
in warm water for 1 hour, drained,
stems discarded, shredded

4 cups (32 fl oz/1 liter) chicken stock

1 tablespoon light soy sauce

1 teaspoon dark soy sauce

½ teaspoon sesame oil

1 tablespoon finely chopped
green (spring) onion

❖ Combine the salt, sugar, 1 teaspoon of the rice wine, the cornstarch, and 1 tablespoon water in a bowl. Add the chicken, toss to coat, and set aside for 15 minutes to marinate.

❖ Bring a saucepan of water to a boil and add the noodles. When the water returns to a boil, add the ⅓ cup (2½ fl oz/80 ml) cold water. Cook for 3–4 minutes, stirring to separate the noodles. Using tongs, transfer the noodles to a colander. Reserve the cooking water. Rinse the noodles under cold water. Return the cooking water to a boil. Return the noodles to the pan and cook for 1 minute more. Drain the noodles and divide among serving bowls; set aside.

❖ Heat the oil in a wok or frying pan. Add the ginger, cabbage, and mushrooms and stir-fry for 30 seconds. Stir in 1 cup (8 fl oz/250 ml) of the broth and cook over medium-low heat for 3 minutes. Stir in the chicken, soy sauces, sesame oil, and remaining rice wine and cook over medium heat for 1½ minutes. Spoon the chicken mixture over the noodles and sprinkle with the green onion.

❖ Bring the remaining 3 cups (24 fl oz/750 ml) of broth to a boil. Pour over the noodles and chicken mixture in each bowl, and serve.

chicken broth
with rice and shrimp

serves 6

7 cups (56 fl oz/1.75 l)
chicken stock

½ cup (3 oz/90 g) white rice,
rinsed well

1 teaspoon salt (optional)

½ cup (4 fl oz/125 ml) olive oil

4 tablespoons chopped cilantro
(fresh coriander)

4 tablespoons finely chopped
fresh serrano chiles

½ cup (4 oz/125 g) finely
chopped tomatoes

8 medium shrimp (prawns),
peeled, cooked, and
finely chopped

1 lime or lemon,
cut into 6 wedges

❖ Bring the stock to a boil in a large saucepan. Add the rice and cook for 15–20 minutes, until it "flowers". (To let it "flower" means to boil it until the grains open and break apart.) Add salt, if desired.

❖ To serve, place the olive oil in a small serving bowl on the table and place each of the remaining ingredients in separate small bowls. Ladle the rice soup into serving bowls and let each person add the other ingredients to taste, squeezing in a few drops of lime or lemon juice just before eating.

port, pear, and fig
casserole

serves 4

3 tablespoons butter

4 chicken drumsticks, skin removed

4 green (spring) onions, chopped

½ cup (4 fl oz/125 ml) dry red wine

½ cup (4 fl oz/125 ml) port

1 cup (8 fl oz/250 ml) chicken stock

2 small pears, quartered

1 tablespoon cornstarch (cornflour)

1 tablespoon cold water

⅔ cup (6 oz/185 g) chunky cranberry sauce

4 fresh figs, quartered

1 tablespoon chopped fresh chives

❖ Melt the butter in a large shallow frying pan. Add the chicken and cook until well browned all over; remove from the pan and set aside. Drain the fat from the pan, add the green onions, wine, port, and stock, and bring to a boil. Add the chicken and any cooking juices to the pan and simmer, covered, for 10 minutes.

❖ Add the pears to the pan and simmer, covered, for 10 minutes more, or until tender. Combine the cornstarch and water in a bowl. Add to the pan and stir until the mixture boils and thickens. Add the cranberry sauce, figs, and chives and stir gently until hot. Serve immediately.

mexican
chile chicken
soup

serves 8–10

1 whole chicken breast, with skin

2 chicken drumsticks, skin removed

2 chicken thighs, skin removed

8 cups (2 qt/2 l) water

1 onion, quartered

½ teaspoon dried oregano

1½ teaspoons salt, or to taste

1 fresh guajillo chile, lightly roasted

2 fresh poblano chiles, lightly roasted

1 lb (500 g) tomatillos, husks removed
(or drained canned tomatillos)

2 cloves garlic, roasted

¼ teaspoon ground cumin

½ cup (2 oz/60 g) masa harina
(tortilla flour)

¼ cup (2 fl oz/60 ml) water

CHOCHOYOTES

½ cup (2 oz/60 g) masa harina
(tortilla flour)

⅓ cup (2½ fl oz/80 ml) warm water

½ tablespoon lard or butter

¼ teaspoon salt, or to taste

purchased flour tortillas (optional)

◈ Combine the chicken pieces, water, onion, oregano, and salt in a large stockpot. Bring to a boil, then reduce the heat, cover, and simmer for 35 minutes, or until the chicken is cooked. Strain the stock into a bowl; reserve. Reserve the chicken and discard the onion and oregano.

◈ When the chicken has cooled, remove the bone and skin from the breast, reserving the skin. Remove the bones from the drumsticks and thighs. Blend the skin from the breast and the meat from the drumsticks and thighs in batches in a blender with 4 cups (32 fl oz/1 liter) of the reserved stock until smooth. Chop the breast meat into bite-sized pieces and place in a large saucepan. Add the blended chicken mixture and stir to combine.

◈ Clean and devein the chiles. Place them in hot water for 10–15 minutes to soften; drain.

◈ If using fresh tomatillos, cook them in water to cover for 10–15 minutes, or until soft; drain. Blend the chiles, cooked or canned tomatillos, garlic, and cumin in a blender until smooth. Add to the saucepan with the remaining reserved stock, stir well, and bring to a simmer.

◈ Dissolve the *masa harina* in the water and gradually add to the pan. Stir constantly with a wooden spatula for 25 minutes, or until the mixture is quite thick.

◈ Meanwhile, for the chochoyotes, mix the masa harina with the warm water to make a soft dough. Add the lard or butter and salt and mix together until well blended. Shape into ¾-inch (2-cm) balls and make a small indentation on 1 side of each with your finger. Add the chochoyotes to the saucepan and cook until heated through. Serve with tortillas, if desired.

family chicken broth

makes 10 cups

2 lb (1 kg) chicken carcass
bones (including necks)

8 oz (250 g) pork shoulder,
leg, loin, or fillet

2 green (spring) onions,
white part only

2 oz (60 g) fresh ginger,
peeled and slightly crushed

salt

✧ Combine all the ingredients in a stockpot and add
enough water to cover the chicken. Bring to a boil,
then reduce the heat and simmer gently, covered,
for 1½ hours.

✧ Strain the broth through a large colander lined with
2 layers of cheesecloth (muslin) into a bowl. Discard the
solids. If using while hot, skim fat. (Or, refrigerate for
several hours or overnight, then lift off the layer of fat.)

✧ Store in an airtight container in the refrigerator for
up to 3 days or in the freezer for up to 6 months.

garnishes

G arnishes add flavor, crunch, visual appeal, and extra nutrition to soups and stews. They are essential additions to some recipes, optional extras to others.

The following list contains hints for various garnishes. Use them as a starting point, but let imagination and personal preference be your ultimate guide. Remember that garnishes should meld with and complement, rather than clash with or overwhelm, the other flavors of the dish.

- Asian sesame oil
- bean sprouts
- bamboo shoots, shredded
- caramelized onion
- chile sauce or Thai hot sauce
- chile oil
- chiles, chopped, with or without seeds (they will be hotter if the seeds are left in)
- cilantro (fresh coriander) leaves, chopped or torn
- crème fraîche
- crisp-fried Chinese noodles

- crisp-fried garlic flakes
- crisp-fried shallot flakes
- croutons
- green (spring) onions, sliced
- guacamole
- harissa
- herbs, chopped (for example, basil goes well with tomato-based or many Italian dishes; dill complements fish; tarragon enhances chicken; coriander complements many Asian recipes)

- mayonnaise (regular or garlic)
- pappadums
- pesto
- red (Spanish) onions, chopped
- sesame seeds, toasted or plain
- shrimp (prawn) crackers
- sour cream
- soy sauce
- tomatoes, diced
- yogurt

supreme chicken broth

makes 12 cups (3 qt/3 l)

1 chicken, 3 lb (1.5 kg)

1 lb (500 g) pork shoulder or loin

2 green (spring) onions, white part only

2 oz (60 g) fresh ginger,
peeled and slightly crushed

2 tablespoons Chinese rice wine
or dry sherry

❖ Place chicken and pork in a stockpot with just enough cold water to cover. Bring to a boil over high heat; skim off the scum. Add onions, ginger, and rice wine or sherry. Reduce heat, cover, and simmer for 2 hours.

❖ Remove solids. Reserve chicken breast meat and discard all other solids. Lightly mash chicken breast meat and reserve. Strain the broth through a colander lined with cheesecloth (muslin). Set aside to cool.

❖ Place the reserved meat and broth in a saucepan over high heat. Stir steadily in one direction (clockwise or counter-clockwise, but do not change direction) until boiling. Reduce heat and boil gently for 15 minutes.

❖ Remove the chicken meat and strain the broth again. Use immediately or store in an airtight container in the refrigerator for up to 3 days or in the freezer for up to 6 months.

chicken soup with potato patties

serves 6

CHICKEN STOCK

1 chicken, 2½ lb (1.25 kg), cut up

3 leafy celery tops

1 yellow onion, quartered

2 cinnamon sticks

2 cardamom pods

SPICE PASTE

3 lemongrass stalks, white part only, coarsely chopped

4 fresh or 2 dried galangal slices, about 1 inch (2.5 cm) in diameter, chopped (if using dried galangal, soak in hot water for 30 minutes, drain, then chop)

1 yellow onion, coarsely chopped

4 cloves garlic

6 candlenuts or blanched almonds

1 piece fresh ginger, 1½ inches (4 cm) long, peeled and coarsely chopped

2 tablespoons ground coriander

1 teaspoon ground pepper

1 teaspoon ground turmeric

2 teaspoons sugar

1 teaspoon salt

3 tablespoons water, approximately

2 tablespoons peanut or corn oil

chicken soup with potato patties

POTATO PATTIES

1 lb (500 g) baking potatoes, peeled, boiled until tender

1 green (spring) onion, finely chopped

½ teaspoon salt

1 egg, lightly beaten

vegetable oil, for frying

◈ For the stock, place the chicken in a large stockpot and add enough water to cover. Bring to a boil over high heat, skimming off any scum. Add the celery tops, onion, cinnamon, and cardamom. Reduce the heat to low, cover partially, and simmer until the chicken is white throughout, about 40 minutes. Transfer the chicken to a plate and allow to cool. Simmer the stock for 20 minutes more, to reduce the volume and concentrate the flavor.

◈ Allow the stock to cool, then strain through a fine-mesh sieve into a bowl. Set aside until the fat rises to the surface. Use a large spoon to skim off the fat. You should have about 8 cups (64 fl oz/2 l) of stock.

◈ Remove the skin and bones from the chicken breasts and shred the meat; set aside. Reserve the remaining chicken pieces for another use.

◈ For the spice paste, place the lemongrass, galangal,

chicken soup with potato patties

onion, garlic, candlenuts or almonds, ginger, coriander, pepper, turmeric, sugar, and salt in a blender. Blend to a smooth paste, adding water as needed to facilitate blending.

◈ Heat the oil in a large saucepan over medium heat. Add the spice paste and cook, stirring often, until well combined and fragrant, about 5 minutes. Stir in the chicken stock and simmer for 15 minutes. Taste and adjust the seasonings, if necessary. Keep warm over low heat.

◈ For the potato patties, combine the potatoes, green onion, salt, and egg in a bowl. Use a potato masher or fork to mash the potato mixture. Shape the mixture into 1-inch (2.5-cm) balls (you should have 12) and flatten each into a patty, 1½ inches (4 cm) in diameter.

◈ Add enough oil to a deep frying pan to reach a depth of 1 inch (2.5 cm). Heat to 375°F (190°C) on a deep-frying thermometer. Add the potato patties, a few at a time, and fry until golden brown underneath, about 3 minutes. Turn the patties and fry until golden brown on the other side, about 1 minute more. Transfer to paper towels to drain. Cover with aluminum foil to keep warm while you fry the remaining patties.

◈ Bring the stock to a simmer. Divide the shredded chicken meat evenly among serving bowls and ladle the hot stock over the top. Place 2 potato patties in each bowl and serve immediately.

1 tablespoon vegetable oil

4 skinless, boneless chicken breast halves, sliced

5 oz (155 g) chorizo (Spanish cured spicy sausage), chopped

2 onions, chopped

2 cloves garlic, crushed

1 tablespoon ground cumin

¼ teaspoon chile powder

3 cups (24 fl oz/750 ml) chicken stock

3 cups (24 fl oz/750 ml) tomato juice

2½ tablespoons tomato paste

2 teaspoons sugar

1 red bell pepper (capsicum), chopped

1 green bell pepper (capsicum), chopped

2 zucchini (courgettes), chopped

1 can (12 oz/375 g) red kidney beans, rinsed, drained

1 can (12 oz/375 g) corn kernels, drained

2½ tablespoons chopped cilantro (fresh coriander)

salt and ground pepper

❖ Heat the oil in a large saucepan over medium heat and cook the chicken and chorizo in batches, stirring, until lightly browned; remove from pan and set aside. Add the onions and garlic to the pan and cook, stirring, until the onions soften. Add the cumin and chile powder and cook, stirring, until fragrant, about 1 minute.

❖ Stir in the stock, tomato juice, tomato paste, and sugar and bring to a boil. Add the bell peppers and zucchini and simmer, uncovered, about 5 minutes or until just tender. Stir in the reserved chicken and chorizo, the beans, corn, and cilantro. Simmer, uncovered, until heated through. Season to taste with salt and pepper.

❖ This soup can be made a day ahead.

spicy chicken and corn soup;
cornmeal muffins (page 265)

spicy chicken
and corn soup

chicken and saffron bouillabaisse

serves 4

¼ cup (2 fl oz/60 ml) olive oil

2 leeks, washed, trimmed, and sliced

2 cloves garlic, crushed

4 chicken drumsticks, skin removed

6 large celery stalks, thickly sliced

1 can (13½ oz/425 g) tomatoes, undrained, crushed

⅓ cup (2½ fl oz/80 ml) Pernod or Ricard

¼ teaspoon powdered saffron or saffron threads

1 tablespoon chopped fresh thyme

2 tablespoons chopped fresh dill

3 cups (24 fl oz/750 ml) chicken stock

Tabasco sauce, to taste

salt and ground pepper, to taste

❖ Combine all ingredients except the stock, Tabasco sauce, salt, and pepper in a large non-metallic dish. Stir well to coat the chicken in the mixture. Cover and refrigerate overnight.

❖ Transfer the chicken and marinade to a large saucepan and bring to a boil. Reduce heat, cover, and simmer for 15 minutes. Stir in the chicken stock and simmer, covered, for a further 15 minutes, or until the chicken is tender and cooked through. Season to taste with Tabasco sauce, salt, and pepper.

❖ This recipe is best prepared a day ahead and then reheated gently just before serving.

thai coconut chicken soup

serves 6–8

8 kaffir lime leaves or
the zest (rind) of 1 lime

2 cans (13½ fl oz/425 ml each)
coconut milk

2 cups (16 fl oz/500 ml) chicken stock

6 fresh or 4 dried galangal slices, each
about 1 inch (2.5 cm) in diameter

4 lemongrass stalks, cut into
2-inch (5-cm) lengths, crushed

4 small fresh green chiles, halved

1 tablespoon Thai roasted chile paste
(nam prik pao)

1 whole chicken breast, skin removed,
cut into ½-inch (1-cm) cubes

½ cup (2½ oz/75 g) drained,
canned whole straw mushrooms

½ cup (2½ oz/75 g) drained,
canned bamboo shoots, sliced

¼ cup (2 fl oz/60 ml)
Thai fish sauce

juice of 2 limes (about
⅓ cup/2½ fl oz/80 ml)

¼ cup (¼ oz/7 g) cilantro
(fresh coriander) leaves

❖ Place 4 of the lime leaves or half of the zest in a large saucepan. Add the coconut milk, chicken stock, galangal, lemongrass, and chiles. Bring to a boil, then reduce heat to low and simmer for 20 minutes. Strain through a fine-mesh sieve into a clean saucepan. Discard the contents of the sieve.

❖ Bring the strained liquid to a boil. Reduce heat until the mixture is boiling gently. Add the remaining lime leaves or zest, chile paste, chicken, mushrooms, bamboo shoots, and fish sauce. Boil gently until the chicken is cooked through, about 3 minutes.

❖ Stir in the lime juice and cilantro, and serve immediately.

257

chicken noodle
vegetable soup

serves 4

6 cups (48 fl oz/1.5 l) chicken stock

1 yellow onion, finely chopped

2 carrots, halved lengthwise, thinly sliced

2 celery stalks, thinly sliced

2 zucchini (courgettes), thinly sliced

2 tablespoons finely chopped fresh parsley

2 oz (60 g) dried very thin egg noodles

½ cup (3 oz/90 g) shredded or cubed, skinless cooked chicken meat

salt and ground pepper

❖ In a large saucepan over medium-low heat, bring the chicken stock to a simmer. Add the onion, carrots, and celery and simmer until the vegetables are slightly soft, about 10 minutes. Add the zucchini and half of the parsley and cook until the zucchini is just tender, about 10 minutes.

❖ Add the noodles and simmer until they are just tender, about 4 minutes, or according to the package directions.

❖ Three minutes before the noodles are done, stir in the chicken. Just before serving, season to taste with salt and pepper. Serve sprinkled with the remaining 1 tablespoon parsley.

hearty chicken soup
with dumplings

serves 6

½ cup (4 oz/125 g) pearl barley

8 oz (250 g) frozen fava (broad) beans

2 tablespoons oil

2 lb (1 kg) skinless chicken
breast halves, sliced

3 leeks, washed, trimmed, and sliced

2 cloves garlic, crushed

3 celery stalks, chopped

3 medium carrots, chopped

2 medium zucchini
(courgettes), chopped

8 cups (2 qt/2 l) chicken stock

½ cup (4 oz/125 g) tomato paste

DUMPLINGS

¼ cup (1½ oz/45 g) yellow
cornmeal (polenta)

¾ cup (3 oz/90 g) all-purpose
(plain) flour

1½ teaspoons baking powder

¼ teaspoon salt

½ cup (2 oz/60 g) grated
Parmesan cheese

¼ cup (2 oz/60 g) butter, grated

½ cup (4 fl oz/125 ml) water,
approximately

⅓ cup (½ oz/15 g) chopped fresh parsley

1 tablespoon chopped fresh thyme

salt and pepper

hearty chicken soup with dumplings

❖ Rinse the barley under cold water until the water runs clear; drain. Pour boiling water over the fava beans, drain, and remove the skins.

❖ Heat the oil in a large saucepan. Cook the chicken in batches until well browned all over. Set aside. Add the leeks, garlic, celery, carrots, and zucchini to the saucepan and cook, stirring, until the leeks are soft, about 10 minutes. Add the chicken stock and tomato paste and bring to a boil. Add the barley and simmer, covered, for 20 minutes. Return the chicken to the pan with the fava beans.

❖ Meanwhile, for the dumplings, combine the polenta, flour, baking powder, salt, cheese, and butter in a bowl. Mix well. Gradually add enough of the water to form a soft dough. Drop level tablespoonfuls of the dumpling mixture into the simmering soup. Cover and simmer for about 15 minutes, or until the dumplings are cooked through and the barley is tender. Stir in the parsley and thyme and season to taste with salt and pepper. Serve immediately.

chinese
combination soup

serves 6–8

8 cups (2 qt/2 l) Family Chicken Broth (page 246)

½ cup (4 oz/125 g) barbecued pork (char sieu, available at Chinese stores), diced

1 skinless chicken breast, diced

½ cup (2 oz/60 g) fresh or drained canned bamboo shoots, finely diced

½ cup (2 oz/60 g) fresh or drained canned water chestnuts, finely diced

¼ cup (1 oz/30 g) fresh white mushrooms (champignons), finely diced

½ cup (4 oz/125 g) fresh green peas

½ teaspoon salt

ground white pepper

1 teaspoon sesame oil

3 tablespoons cornstarch (cornflour), mixed with a little cold water

2 oz (60 g) uncooked shrimp (green prawns), peeled, deveined, and diced

2 fresh bean curd squares, diced

❖ Bring the chicken broth to a boil. Add all of the ingredients, except the cornstarch mixture, shrimp, and bean curd. Simmer for 15 minutes.

❖ Add the cornstarch mixture to the soup, stirring constantly until the soup returns to a boil and thickens slightly.

❖ Stir in the shrimp and bean curd and cook for 1 minute. Serve hot.

chicken broth
with avocado and tortillas

serves 8

½ cup (4 fl oz/125 ml)
vegetable oil

6 purchased tortillas,
cut into thin strips

8 cups (64 fl oz/2 l)
chicken stock

1 chicken breast half,
cooked and shredded

1 fresh serrano chile,
seeded and chopped

squeeze of lime juice

1 teaspoon salt, or to taste

1 large avocado, peeled, stone
removed, flesh sliced or cubed

2 tablespoons cilantro (fresh
coriander), roughly chopped

✦ Heat the oil in a frying pan. Add the tortilla strips
and cook until crisp. Drain on paper towels.

✦ Place the stock, chicken, chile, lime juice, and salt in
a saucepan. Cook over medium heat until very hot.

✦ Place the avocado and tortilla strips in separate
bowls to pass around at the table. Serve the hot soup
sprinkled with the cilantro.

cornmeal muffins

makes 8 muffins

1 cup (6 oz/185 g) yellow
cornmeal (polenta)

½ cup (2 oz/60 g) all-purpose
(plain) flour

1½ teaspoons baking powder

2 teaspoons sugar

½ teaspoon salt

2 eggs, lightly beaten

½ cup (4 fl oz/125 ml)
buttermilk

⅓ cup (2½ oz/80 g)
butter, melted

1 small can (4½ oz/140 g)
corn kernels, drained

¾ cup (3 oz/90 g) grated
Cheddar cheese

❖ Preheat an oven to 400°F (200°C/Gas Mark 5). Grease eight ⅓-cup (2½ fl oz/80-ml) muffin pans. Combine the polenta, flour, baking powder, sugar, and salt in a large bowl. Add the eggs, buttermilk, butter, corn, and cheese and mix well to combine. Spoon the mixture into the greased pans and bake for 25 minutes, or until a skewer inserted in the centers of the muffins comes out clean. Allow to cool in the tins for a few minutes before turning out onto a wire rack. Serve hot or warm, with your favorite soup or stew.

cantonese
noodle soup

serves 6

2 tablespoons light soy sauce

salt and ground black pepper

2 teaspoons cornstarch (cornflour)

1 whole skinless chicken breast,
cut into julienne strips

4 oz (125 g) pork fillet, loin, or shoulder,
cut into julienne strips

2 tablespoons peanut oil

2 slices fresh ginger, shredded

1 clove garlic, finely chopped

6 dried shiitake mushrooms, soaked for
45 minutes in warm water, drained,
stems discarded, caps cut in half

½ cup (2 oz/60 g) drained canned
bamboo shoots, thinly sliced

1 cup (2 oz/60 g) roughly torn green
vegetables, such as lettuce, spinach,
or Chinese cabbage

6 cups (48 fl oz/1.5 l) Supreme
Chicken Broth (page 248)

12 oz (375 g) dried, fresh, or yi-fu noodles
(see note for preparing noodles, opposite)

1 teaspoon sesame oil

¼ cup (½ oz/15 g) green (spring) onions,
shredded, for garnish

cilantro (fresh coriander), roughly broken
into 3-inch (7.5-cm) lengths, for garnish

✥ Combine the soy sauce, salt, pepper, and cornstarch in a bowl. Add the chicken and pork, toss to coat thoroughly, and set aside to marinate while you prepare the other ingredients.

✥ Heat the peanut oil in a wok until it is just smoking. Add the ginger and garlic and stir-fry for 2 minutes (take care not to burn them). Add the drained chicken and pork and stir-fry until the meat changes color from pink to white. Add the mushrooms, bamboo shoots, and green vegetables and stir-fry for 10 seconds. Add about 2 tablespoons of the broth and stir-fry over high heat for 1 minute. Transfer to a bowl and set aside.

✥ Bring half of the remaining broth to a boil in a saucepan. Add the prepared noodles and cook for 1 minute. Transfer to a soup tureen.

✥ Bring the remaining chicken broth to a boil in a saucepan. Add the vegetable mixture and return to a boil. Add to the soup tureen. Sprinkle with the sesame oil. Serve garnished with the green onions and cilantro.

preparing noodles

dried noodles Add to boiling water and stir well. Add a little sesame oil. Return to a boil and boil for 4–5 minutes (or as directed on the package). Drain and rinse under cold running water. Drain and set aside.

fresh noodles Follow instructions for dried noodles, but cook for 1–2 minutes (or as directed on the package).

yi-fu noodles These are boiled, then deep-fried and packaged. They are rich in flavour with a smooth, fluffy texture. Follow instructions for dried noodles, but cook for 1–2 minutes (depending on package directions).

turkey black bean chili
with ancho salsa

serves 6

Some food scholars say that chile-seasoned stews of meat and beans belong more to Texas and the American Southwest than to Mexico. Certainly, this is a cantina dish of the northern borderlands, and it owes a debt to present-day sensibilities in its health-conscious combination of ground turkey and black beans.

2 cups (14 oz/440 g) dried black beans

8 cups (64 fl oz/2 l) water

2 fresh árbol chiles

3 bay leaves

ANCHO SALSA

4 dried ancho chiles, stemmed and seeded

½ cup (4 fl oz/125 ml) fresh orange juice

¼ cup (2 fl oz/60 ml) fresh lime juice

1 teaspoon salt

2 tablespoons extra virgin olive oil

2 tablespoons vegetable oil

1 lb (500 g) coarsely ground (minced) turkey

1 large yellow onion, diced

1 teaspoon salt, or to taste

1/2 teaspoon ground black pepper

1/2 teaspoon cayenne pepper

3 cloves garlic, finely chopped

2 fresh poblano chiles, stemmed, seeded, and diced

1 1/2 tablespoons chile powder

1 1/2 tablespoons ground cumin

2 cups (16 fl oz/500 ml) chicken stock, or as needed

Sort through the beans and discard any misshapen beans or stones. Rinse well. Combine the beans, water, árbol chiles, and bay leaves in a large saucepan and bring to a boil. Reduce the heat to medium, cover, and simmer until tender, about 1 hour. Discard the chiles and bay leaves. Drain the bean mixture and set aside.

Meanwhile, for the ancho salsa, toast the ancho chiles in a cast-iron frying pan over medium heat, turning often to avoid scorching, until soft and brown, 1–2 minutes. Remove from the heat, chop, and place in a bowl. Add the orange juice, lime juice, salt, and olive oil. Mix well and set aside at room temperature for at least 30 minutes or up to 2 hours before serving. (The salsa can be covered and refrigerated for up to 2 days.)

Heat the vegetable oil in a large saucepan over medium heat. Add the turkey and cook, stirring often, until browned, about 10 minutes. Add the onion, salt, black pepper, and cayenne pepper and cook, stirring occasionally, until light golden, about 10 minutes.

turkey black bean chili with ancho salsa

Add the garlic, poblano chiles, chile powder, and cumin and cook, stirring, until fragrant, 2–3 minutes.

◈ Add the black bean mixture and 2 cups (16 fl oz/ 500 ml) chicken stock and cook, uncovered, until the flavors have blended and the mixture has thickened, 30–40 minutes. Taste and adjust the seasonings, adding more chicken stock if needed.

◈ Ladle the chile into serving bowls and top each serving with a dollop of ancho salsa.

recipe hint

Ancho chiles are mild, full-flavored, deep-purple to black chiles that are arguably the most popular dried chiles used in Mexican cooking. When they are fresh and green, they are known as poblano chiles.

yin-yang soup

serves 4

YANG SOUP

1 bunch spinach, stalks removed

4 cups (32 fl oz/1 liter) Supreme
Chicken Broth (page 248)

1 teaspoon fish sauce

½ teaspoon cornstarch (cornflour),
mixed with 3 tablespoons cold water

peanut oil

YIN SOUP

1 cup (8 fl oz/250 ml) chicken stock

½ cup (4 fl oz/125 ml) cold water

1 whole skinless chicken breast,
ground (minced)

few drops of fish sauce

few drops of sesame oil

1 teaspoon cornstarch (cornflour),
mixed with 1 tablespoon cold water

2 egg whites

yin-yang soup

❖ For the Yang soup, wash the spinach leaves thoroughly and blanch in boiling water until they soften. Rinse under cold water, drain well, and finely chop to make a rough purée.

❖ Heat the broth in a saucepan. Add the spinach and heat through. Add the fish sauce and stir in enough of the cornstarch mixture to make a soup that is velvety thick. Stir in a dash of peanut oil. Ladle into a serving bowl.

❖ For the Yin soup, heat the stock in a saucepan until it is almost boiling, then remove from the heat and allow to cool a little. Meanwhile, add the cold water to the chicken and beat by hand to mix well. Add the chicken mixture to the broth and stir quickly over medium heat to prevent lumping and to distribute the pieces.

❖ Add the fish sauce and sesame oil. Stir in enough of the cornstarch mixture to give the soup a light "holding" consistency (the liquid should hold onto the back of a spoon but run off at the same time).

❖ Add the egg whites, stirring gently and swirling the saucepan to cook the eggs evenly.

❖ Carefully spoon the yin soup over the yang soup to make a curving Yin-Yang symbol. Dot the white chicken soup with a little of the green spinach soup, and the green spinach soup with a little of the white chicken soup. Serve immediately.

winter melon soup

8 cups (64 fl oz/2 l) water

2 chicken thighs, with bones

2 chicken drumsticks

small piece of ham bone
or bacon bone

l lb (500 g) winter melon,
fuzzy melon (dit qwar), or
English chock (available
at Chinese stores)

4 dried Chinese oysters,
mussels, or clams
(available at Chinese stores)

1 tablespoon Tianjin red beans
(hong dow, available
at Chinese stores)

◈ Combine the water, chicken pieces, and ham or bacon bone in a large stockpot. Bring to a simmer and simmer for 1 hour.

◈ Cut the melon or chock into 1½-inch (4-cm) chunks, keeping the skin on for maximum flavor.

◈ Rinse the dried oysters, mussels, or clams, and the Tianjin red beans. Add to the chicken broth with the melon or chock and simmer for 1 hour more.

◈ Before serving, remove the chicken pieces and ham or bacon bone and serve in a separate dish.

microwave
soups and stews

oyster soup

serves 4

1 tablespoon butter

2 tablespoons all-purpose (plain) flour

2 cups (16 fl oz/500 ml) chicken stock

1 cup (8 fl oz/250 ml) fish stock or water

1/2 cup (4 fl oz/125 ml) cream

24 bottled oysters, well drained

ground white pepper

snipped fresh chives, for garnish

✧ Place the butter and flour in an 8-cup (2-qt/2-l) microwave-safe dish or casserole. Heat on high (100%) for 1 minute, stirring after 30 seconds. Add the chicken stock and fish stock or water, and stir well. Cook on high for 5–6 minutes, stirring every minute, until the liquid boils and thickens.

✧ Stir in the cream, oysters, and pepper to taste. Cook on medium (50%) for 1–2 minutes, until the ingredients are heated through.

✧ Serve immediately, sprinkled with the chives.

cooking soups in the
microwave

M any soups take a long time to cook by conventional means, but that time is greatly reduced when the microwave oven is used. Remember when cooking soup in the microwave to use a large cooking container, preferably one that is deep with straight sides. Stir well and often, to ensure that ingredients cook evenly and that the soup doesn't boil over.

If converting your own recipes for the microwave, remember that very little evaporation takes place, so cut down on any liquid by one-third. Shorten cooking time by always adding hot or boiling water or stock, and never season with salt until cooking is complete. When adding herbs, keep in mind that their flavors are a

little more concentrated when used in microwave recipes.

It is difficult to be precise in giving cooking times for microwave ovens, as individual ovens vary. The golden rule is to undercook the food, then check to see if it is done and return it to the oven if necessary. If it is almost cooked, any further cooking should be done in bursts of a few seconds only to avoid overcooking.

The recipes in this book are designed for a 650-watt oven. Ovens with less power will need a little more time and those with more power less time. The table below will serve as a quick reference. If in doubt, always be guided by your oven's instruction manual.

quick microwave stock

Stock for soups can be quickly made by cooking meat or chicken scraps and bones with seasonings (such as chopped carrot, onion, and celery, and a bouquet garni, bay leaf, or other herbs) and water. For each 2 cups (16 fl oz/500 ml) of liquid, allow 5 minutes on high (100%), then 10 minutes on medium (50%). Set aside for 10 minutes, then strain. If using the stock immediately, skim off any fat by drawing a paper towel over the top of the hot stock to blot up fat. Repeat until all fat is removed. Or, chill the soup then use a large spoon to lift off the layer of fat. The stock may be refrigerated, covered, for up to 3 days or frozen for up to 3 months.

microwave timing

Power	Change of Timing per Minute (+ or –)
900 watts	– 40 seconds
850 watts	– 30 seconds
800 watts	– 20 seconds
750 watts	– 10 seconds
700 watts	– 5 seconds
650 watts	no change
600 watts	+ 5 seconds
550 watts	+ 10 seconds
500 watts	+ 20 seconds
450 watts	+ 30 seconds

shrimp bisque

serves 4–6

10 oz (315 g) peeled uncooked shrimp (green prawns)

1 tablespoon butter

1 small onion, finely chopped

1 small carrot, peeled and grated or finely chopped

1 celery stalk, chopped

1 tablespoon tomato purée

½ cup (3 oz/90 g) long-grain white rice

1 bouquet garni

¼ cup (2 fl oz/60 ml) white wine

2 tablespoons brandy

4 cups (32 fl oz/1 liter) fish stock

salt and ground black pepper

2 tablespoons cream

croutons, to serve (optional)

❖ Devein the shrimp. Melt the butter in a 12-cup (3-qt/3-l) microwave-safe dish or casserole on high (100%) for 45 seconds. Add the prawns and toss well to coat. Cook on high for 1 minute. Stir in the onion, carrot, and celery. Cover with a well-fitting lid or plastic wrap and cook on high for 2–3 minutes.

❖ Stir in the tomato purée, rice, bouquet garni, white wine, brandy, and half of the stock. Cover and cook on high for 10–12 minutes, until the rice is tender.

❖ Remove 4 prawns; set aside. Discard bouquet garni. Purée the soup in a blender or food processor. Return to the casserole. Dilute to the required consistency with the remaining stock. Add salt and pepper to taste.

❖ Heat on high for 2–3 minutes. Stir in the cream. Ladle into serving bowls and serve garnished with a reserved prawn and some croutons, if desired.

split pea and bacon soup

serves 6–8

1½ cups (10 oz/315 g) green split peas

9 cups (2¼ qt/2.25 l) water

2 bacon rashers, chopped

1 large onion, chopped

1 large carrot, peeled, chopped

1 celery stalk, chopped

1 medium potato, chopped

2 bacon stock cubes

½ teaspoon dried thyme

½ teaspoon ground pepper

1 bay leaf

8 oz (250 g) bacon bones

salt

1 cooked bacon rasher, crumbled, for garnishing

❖ Place the peas in a 16-cup (4-qt/4-l) microwave-safe casserole with 4 cups (32 fl oz/1 liter) of the water. Cook on high (100%) for 10 minutes, stirring halfway through cooking. Cover and set aside. Place the bacon in a smaller casserole and cook on high for 1 minute. Stir in the onion, carrot, celery, and potato and cook, covered, on high for 5 minutes. Crumble the stock cubes into the casserole containing the peas and add the remaining water, vegetable mixture, thyme, pepper, bay leaf, bacon bones, and salt. Stir well and cook on high for 25 minutes, stirring twice during cooking.

❖ Remove the bacon bones and return any meat to the soup. Discard the bay leaf. Blend the soup, if desired. Serve garnished with the crumbled bacon.

mediterranean seafood soup

serves 4–6

2 teaspoons butter

1 large onion, sliced

3 leeks, washed and thinly sliced

2 carrots, peeled and thinly sliced

1 celery stalk, thinly sliced

1 green bell pepper (capsicum),
seeded and thinly sliced

4 cups (32 fl oz/1 liter) water, fish stock, or
diluted chicken stock, boiling

1 bay leaf

1 teaspoon dried thyme

4 sprigs fresh parsley

pinch of powdered saffron

2 cloves garlic, crushed

6 fish steaks (such as gemfish or kingfish)

3½ oz (105 g) peeled uncooked shrimp
(green prawns)

6 fresh oysters, shelled (or fresh
bottled oysters, drained)

salt and ground black pepper

❖ Melt the butter in a 12-cup (3-qt/3-l) microwave-safe casserole on high (100%) for 45 seconds. Add the onion, leeks, carrots, celery, and bell pepper. Stir well to coat. Cover and cook on high for 5 minutes.

❖ Stir in the boiling water or stock. Add the bay leaf, thyme, parsley, saffron, and garlic. Stir to combine, cover, and cook on high for 5 minutes. (The water or stock must be boiling when it is added to the vegetables so it will quickly bring out flavors that would otherwise take a while to extract.)

❖ Stir well, then add the fish steaks. Cover and cook on high for 5 minutes. Stir in the prawns and oysters. Cook on high for 1 minute more. Taste and adjust the seasonings, if necessary.

❖ Serve immediately with crusty bread.

seafood secrets

When cooking fish fillets in the microwave, it is important to ensure even cooking. If the fillets have a thin, tapering end, place them in the cooking dish so the thin ends are in the center of the dish, or tuck the ends under themselves or other pieces of fish to avoid overcooking.

To ensure the best possible results, always cover fish, especially fillets, to lessen moisture loss. Check the fish a little before the specified cooking time and remove from the oven when the flesh will *barely* flake when tested with a fork.

curried pumpkin soup

serves 4

1 kg (2 lb) pumpkin, peeled and diced

2 cups (16 fl oz/500 ml) water

1 chicken stock cube or 1 heaped teaspoon stock powder

1 clove garlic, crushed

1 teaspoon curry powder

ground black pepper

2/3 cup (5 fl oz/160 ml) heavy (double) cream

croutons, for serving

ground nutmeg

sprig of fresh tarragon, for garnish

❖ Place the pumpkin in a 12-cup (3-qt/3-l) microwave-safe dish or casserole. Add the water, stock cube or stock powder, garlic, and curry powder. Cover with a well-fitting lid or plastic wrap and cook on high (100%) for 12–14 minutes, stirring after 6 minutes, until the pumpkin breaks down.

❖ Set aside for 3 minutes to cool slightly, then purée the pumpkin mixture in a blender or food processor until smooth. Return to the casserole. Taste and adjust the seasoning, if necessary, and stir in the cream. Cook, uncovered, on high for 4–5 minutes to heat through.

❖ Serve sprinkled with croutons and nutmeg, and garnished with the sprig of tarragon.

hearty tomato and zucchini soup

serves 6

1½ lb (750 g) tomatoes, peeled and chopped

4 medium zucchini (courgettes), thinly sliced

4 cups (32 fl oz/1 liter) chicken stock, boiling

1 tablespoon all-purpose (plain) flour

ground black pepper

2 tablespoons butter

1 teaspoon ground nutmeg

1 tablespoon chopped fresh parsley

1 tablespoon chopped fresh dill

½ cup (4 fl oz/125 ml) sour cream

❖ Place the tomatoes, zucchini, and half of the boiling stock in a 12-cup (3-qt/3-l) microwave-safe dish or casserole. Cook on high (100%) for 10 minutes, stirring occasionally, until the soup comes to the boil. Cook on medium (50%) for 10 minutes more, until the vegetables soften. Set aside.

❖ Place the flour, pepper, and butter in a small bowl. Cook on high for 1 minute, stirring after 30 seconds. Stir in the nutmeg, parsley, and dill. Pour a little of the soup into the bowl and stir to combine. Add to the dish or casserole with the remaining stock and stir well. Cook on high for 3–4 minutes, until the soup returns to a boil and thickens slightly.

❖ Serve immediately, with crusty Italian bread and garnished with sour cream.

microwave beef and vegetable soup

serves 8–10

1 lb (500 g) ground (minced) beef steak

1 large onion, chopped

8 cups (64 fl oz/2 l) beef stock

1 cup (5 oz/155 g) macaroni

1 large potato, chopped

1 large carrot, peeled and chopped

2 celery stalks, chopped

1 tablespoon chopped fresh parsley

1 cup (3 oz/90 g) shredded cabbage

4 large cooking tomatoes, peeled and chopped

½ teaspoon dried oregano or marjoram

salt and ground black pepper

½ cup (2½ oz/75 g) frozen peas (optional)

◈ Place the ground steak in a 16-cup (4-qt/4-l) microwave-safe casserole. Break up the meat with a fork and add the onion. Cover and cook on medium-high (70%) for 6 minutes. Stir well and cook on medium-high for 6 minutes more.

◈ Add the remaining ingredients, except for the peas, and cook on medium-high for 25 minutes. (Stir in the peas, if using, after 15 minutes.) Set aside, covered, for 15 minutes to cool slightly.

◈ Before serving, skim off any fat by drawing a paper towel over the surface of the soup. Repeat until all fat is removed.

beetroot and orange soup

1 lb (500 g) fresh beetroot, peeled, diced

finely grated zest (rind) and juice of 1 orange

2 cups (16 fl oz/500 ml) hot chicken stock

1 cup (8 fl oz/250 ml) tomato juice

ground black pepper

1/3 cup (2 1/2 fl oz/80 ml) sour cream

snipped fresh chives

❖ Place the beetroot in a 12-cup (3-qt/3-l) microwave-safe casserole. Cover with a well-fitting lid or plastic wrap and cook on high (100%) for 6–8 minutes, until tender. Set aside for 5 minutes to cool slightly.

❖ Purée the beetroot and any cooking liquid in a food processor or blender until smooth.

❖ Return the beetroot purée to the casserole. Add the orange zest and juice, stock, tomato juice, and pepper and stir well. Cook on high for 5 minutes, stirring occasionally, until the mixture boils. Cook on medium (50%) for 5 minutes more, stirring occasionally, until the soup is thick and well combined.

❖ This soup may be served hot or chilled. If serving chilled, set aside until cool, then refrigerate for several hours. Serve topped with the sour cream and chives.

gingered carrot soup

serves 4–5

1¼ lb (625 g) carrots,
peeled and sliced

2 cups (16 fl oz/500 ml) hot
chicken stock

finely grated zest (rind)
and juice of 2 oranges

1 cup (8 fl oz/250 ml) water

1 teaspoon ground ginger

½ teaspoon ground mace

⅔ cup (5 fl oz/160 ml) cream

ground black pepper

❖ Place the carrots in a 12-cup (3-qt/3-l) microwave-safe dish or casserole. Cover with a lid or plastic wrap and cook on high (100%) for 5–6 minutes, until soft. Stir in the hot stock, orange zest and juice, water, ginger, and mace. Cook on high for 6–8 minutes, stirring occasionally, until the liquid boils.

❖ Set aside for 5 minutes to cool slightly. Purée the soup in batches in a blender or food processor.

❖ Transfer the soup to an airtight container and stir in half of the cream. Taste and adjust the seasonings, if necessary, and place in the refrigerator to chill.

❖ Serve well chilled, garnished with a spoonful of the remaining cream.

mushroom soup

serves 4–6

2 tablespoons butter

½ cup (1½ oz/45 g) finely chopped green (spring) onions

2 cups (6 oz/185 g) fresh mushrooms, finely chopped

1½ cups (12 fl oz/375 ml) chicken stock

1½ cups (12 fl oz/375 ml) milk

1 tablespoon all-purpose (plain) flour

⅓ cup (2½ fl oz/80 ml) cream

1 egg yolk

chopped fresh chives

lemon slices (optional)

❖ Place the butter, onions, and mushrooms in a deep 12-cup (3-qt/3-l) microwave-safe casserole or dish. Cover and cook on high (100%) for 3 minutes. Stir in the stock and milk. Cook on high for 3 minutes, or until the mixture is bubbling around the edges.

❖ Combine the flour with a little water to make a smooth paste. Stir into the soup and cook on high for 2 minutes. Whisk the cream and egg yolk together in a small jug. Stir in a little of the hot soup, then stir the cream mixture into the soup. Cook on high for 3 minutes or until the soup is bubbling around the edges. Stir well, and serve sprinkled with chives and topped with a slice of lemon, if desired.

indian cauliflower soup

serves 6

2 cups (4 oz/125 g) small cauliflower florets

2 tablespoons butter

½ medium red bell pepper (capsicum), seeded and cut into thin strips

1 large onion, finely chopped

2 teaspoons ground turmeric

½ teaspoon chile powder, or to taste

2 cups (16 fl oz/500 ml) hot chicken stock

1 cup (8 fl oz/250 ml) milk

2 tablespoons besan (chickpea/garbanzo bean flour)

¾ cup (6 oz/185 g) natural yogurt

1 teaspoon garam masala

2 tablespoons chopped cilantro (fresh coriander) or fresh parsley

❖ Make a small cut in each cauliflower floret stem. Melt the butter in a large casserole on high (100%). Add cauliflower, bell pepper, and onion. Cook, covered, on high for 5 minutes, stirring after 3 minutes.

❖ Stir in turmeric, chile powder, and stock. Cook, covered, on high for 8 minutes, stirring often. Meanwhile, add a little of the milk to the *besan* to make a paste. Gradually stir in the remaining milk, then stir the *besan* mixture into the soup. Cover and cook on high until just boiling. Stir in the yogurt and garam masala. Heat on high until almost boiling. Stir in cilantro or parsley, and serve immediately.

french onion soup

2 tablespoons butter

2 large onions, sliced

1 tablespoon all-purpose
(plain) flour

3 cups (24 fl oz/750 ml)
beef stock

¼ cup (2 fl oz/60 ml)
white wine

1 bay leaf

salt and ground black pepper

4 thick slices French bread

2 oz (60 g) Gruyère or
Cheddar cheese, grated

◈ Melt the butter in an 8-cup (2-qt/2-l) microwave-safe casserole on high (100%). Stir in the onions and cook, covered, on high for 5 minutes. Stir in the flour and cook, covered, on high for 1 minute. Gradually stir in the stock, wine, bay leaf, and pepper. Cook on high for 10 minutes. Season with salt, if desired. Discard the bay leaf.

◈ Meanwhile, sprinkle the slices of bread with the grated cheese. Place under a hot broiler (griller) until the cheese melts. Ladle the soup into serving bowls and place a slice of toast on top of each. Serve immediately.

minestrone

1 can (10 oz/315 g) four-bean mix, drained

2 tablespoons olive oil

1 large onion, finely chopped

2 cloves garlic, crushed

2 medium potatoes, peeled and diced

2 medium carrots, peeled and sliced

2 celery stalks, sliced

2 cups (6 oz/185 g) shredded cabbage

3 tomatoes, peeled and chopped

4 cups (32 fl oz/1 liter) hot chicken stock

1 bouquet garni

1 cup (5 oz/155 g) small macaroni

3 oz (90 g) ham off the bone, diced

½ teaspoon paprika

ground black pepper, to taste

1 medium zucchini (courgette), diced

½ cup (2 oz/60 g) grated Parmesan cheese

sprigs of fresh thyme, for garnish

❖ Rinse the four-bean mix; drain. Heat the oil in a 16-cup (4-qt/4-l) microwave-safe casserole on high (100%) for 1–2 minutes, until hot. Stir in the onion and garlic and cook, covered, on high for 2 minutes. Stir in the potatoes, carrots, and celery and cook, covered, on high for 5 minutes.

❖ Stir in the cabbage and tomatoes, then stir in the hot stock, bouquet garni, beans, macaroni, ham, paprika, and pepper. Cook, covered, on high for 20 minutes, stirring after every 5 minutes, until the vegetables and macaroni are tender. Stir well.

❖ Discard the bouquet garni and stir in the zucchini. Cook on high for 5 minutes. Serve sprinkled with the cheese and thyme.

thick lentil soup

serves 4

1 cup (6 oz/185 g)
brown lentils, washed

1 tablespoon butter

1 large onion, finely chopped

1 clove garlic, crushed

1 large carrot, peeled
and thinly sliced

4 cups (32 fl oz/1 liter)
boiling water

1 tablespoon chicken
stock powder

ground black pepper

pinch of ground allspice

1 tablespoon chopped
fresh parsley

❖ Soak the lentils in enough water to cover while preparing the remaining ingredients; drain.

❖ Melt the butter in a 12-cup (3-qt/3-l) microwave-safe casserole or dish on high (100%). Stir in the onion, garlic, and carrot. Cover with a well-fitting lid or plastic wrap and cook on high for 2 minutes. Stir in the lentils and cook, covered, on high for 2 minutes. Stir in the boiling water, stock powder, pepper, allspice, and parsley. Cook, uncovered, on medium (50%) for 15–20 minutes, until the lentils are soft.

❖ Serve immediately. Or, if desired, purée the soup in a blender or food processor, then return to the casserole and heat through before serving.

potato-topped fish casserole

serves 4

1¼ lb (625 g) fish fillets (such as perch or hake), skinned

2 large potatoes, peeled and chopped

2 tablespoons butter

2 bacon rashers, chopped

½ cup (2 oz/60 g) grated Cheddar cheese

1 onion, thinly sliced

1 celery stalk, chopped

3 oz (90 g) fresh button mushrooms, sliced

4 tomatoes, quartered

1 tablespoon Worcestershire sauce

ground black pepper

◈ Cut the fish fillets into large pieces; set aside. Place the potatoes in a microwave-safe bowl. Cover and cook on high (100%) for 6 minutes, until tender. Add half of the butter and use a potato masher to mash well.

◈ Place the bacon between 2 sheets of paper towel. Cook on high for 2 minutes. Stir the bacon and cheese into the mashed potato. Set aside.

◈ Melt remaining butter in a large microwave-safe casserole on high. Stir in onion and celery. Cover and cook on high for 2 minutes. Stir in fish, mushrooms, tomatoes, sauce, and pepper. Cook, covered, on medium-high (70%) for 3 minutes, stirring once.

◈ Top the fish mixture with the potato mixture. Cook, uncovered, on medium-high for 10 minutes. Serve.

turkey casserole with mushrooms

serves 4

2 tablespoons butter

2 tablespoons all-purpose (plain) flour

1 chicken stock cube, crumbled

ground black pepper

½ cup (4 fl oz/125 ml) water

1½ cups (12 fl oz/375 ml) heavy (double) cream

3 cups (15 oz/470 g) cooked pasta shells

2 cups (8 oz/250 g) cooked, diced turkey meat

4 oz (125 g) fresh mushrooms, sliced

1 tablespoon chopped fresh parsley

2 tablespoons sherry

2 tablespoons each of grated Parmesan and Cheddar cheese, combined

❖ Melt the butter in an 8-cup (2-qt/2-l) microwave-safe casserole on high (100%). Stir in the flour, stock cube, and pepper. Gradually stir in the water and cream. Cook on high for 5–6 minutes, stirring often, until the sauce boils and thickens.

❖ Stir in the pasta, turkey, mushrooms, parsley, and sherry. Sprinkle with the combined grated cheeses and cook on medium-high (70%) for 8–10 minutes, until the cheese melts and the casserole is heated through. Serve immediately.

chili con carne

serves 4

12 oz (375 g) lean ground (minced) beef

1 large onion, sliced

*1 green bell pepper (capsicum),
seeded and sliced*

2 cloves garlic, crushed

½–1 teaspoon chile powder, or to taste

1 can (13½ oz/425 g) diced tomatoes

2 tablespoons tomato paste

½ teaspoon dried oregano

*1 can (10 oz/315 g) red kidney beans,
washed, drained*

*cooked macaroni or white rice, or corn
chips, to serve*

❖ Heat a microwave-safe browning dish on high (100%) for 6 minutes, until hot. Add the beef and stir quickly until the sizzling stops. Stir in the onion, bell pepper, garlic, and chile powder to taste. Cover and cook on high for 5 minutes. Stir in the undrained tomatoes, tomato paste, oregano, and kidney beans. Cook on medium (50%) for 20 minutes, until the meat is cooked. Adjust the seasoning with additional chile powder, if desired.

❖ Serve hot, on a bed of cooked macaroni or white rice, or with corn chips.

swiss potato casserole

1½ lb (750 g) red (pontiac) potatoes,
unpeeled, thinly sliced

2 medium carrots, peeled and thinly sliced

2 medium zucchini (courgettes),
thinly sliced

1 cup (4 oz/125 g) grated Swiss cheese

¼ cup (¾ oz/25 g) thinly sliced
green (spring) onion

1 tablespoon chopped fresh basil or parsley

salt and ground black pepper

1 tablespoon butter, melted

¾ cup (6 fl oz/185 ml) tomato juice

½ cup (2 oz/60 g) grated
Swiss cheese, extra

❖ Place a third of the potato slices in a greased 8-inch (20-cm) microwave-safe dish and top with half of the carrot and zucchini slices. Sprinkle with half of the cheese, green onion, and basil or parsley. Season with salt and pepper. Repeat this entire process. Top with the remaining potatoes, and brush with the melted butter. Gently pour the tomato juice over the top.

❖ Cook, covered, on high (100%) for 16–18 minutes, or until the potatoes are tender. Sprinkle with the extra cheese, cover and cook on high for 1 minute more.

❖ Set aside for 5 minutes to cool slightly before serving.

soups
served
chilled

corn soup
with fish roe

serves 8

kernels from 4 corn cobs

4 cups (32 fl oz/1 liter)
chicken stock

1 onion, coarsely chopped

1 bay leaf

pinch each of fresh thyme
and oregano

3 gray mullet roe or any other
hard roe, well washed

boiling water

pinch of ground nutmeg

1 cup (8 fl oz/250 ml)
heavy (double) cream

1 large fresh poblano chile,
roasted, peeled, seeded, and
cut into strips, for garnish

❖ Place the corn kernels and stock in a large saucepan and cook over medium heat for 10 minutes, or until the corn is tender. Place the onion, herbs, and roe in a separate saucepan and add enough boiling water to cover. Cook over medium heat for 7 minutes. Drain, discarding the water and herbs. Peel the roe, discarding the skin, and then break up the roe with a fork.

❖ Place the corn mixture and onion in a blender and roughly blend. Return the mixture to the large saucepan and stir in the nutmeg, cream, and roe. Simmer for a few minutes to blend the flavors.

❖ Refrigerate until cold. Serve garnished with chile.

iced tomato soup

serves 4

2 lb (1 kg) ripe tomatoes, peeled, seeded, and coarsely chopped

1 cup (8 fl oz/250 ml) chicken stock

¼ cup (2 fl oz/60 ml) extra virgin olive oil

⅓ cup (2½ fl oz/80 ml) aged wine vinegar

1 clove garlic, crushed

salt and ground black pepper

4 teaspoons thick crème fraîche

12 small fresh basil leaves

❖ Place the tomatoes, stock, oil, vinegar, garlic, and salt and pepper to taste in a food processor. Process on high for 2 minutes, or until the mixture is smooth. Refrigerate until ready to serve.

❖ Serve topped with a teaspoon of crème fraîche and some basil leaves.

chilled
chicken
and avocado soup

serves 4

3 very ripe avocados

6 teaspoons fresh lemon juice

4 cups (32 fl oz/1 liter) homemade chicken stock, chilled

salt and ground black pepper

❖ Halve the avocados and remove the stones. Working quickly, peel the avocados, then place them in a large bowl and mash the flesh with a fork.

❖ Stir the lemon juice into the avocado purée to prevent the avocado from discoloring.

❖ Add the chicken stock and stir to combine.

❖ Serve immediately, sprinkled with salt and pepper.

smooth gazpacho

serves 4

This soup takes advantage
of a variety of fresh summer
vegetables, combining them
to make a light and
refreshing chilled soup.
Serve with a loaf of crusty
Italian bread for a more
substantial meal.

6 vine-ripened tomatoes

1 1/2 cups (7 1/2 oz/235 g) finely diced cucumber

3/4 cup (4 oz/125 g) finely diced celery

3/4 cup (4 oz/125 g) finely diced
green bell pepper (capsicum)

2/3 cup (3 1/2 oz/105 g) peeled and finely diced carrot

1/2 cup (2 1/2 oz/75 g) finely diced white onion

1/3 cup (1/2 oz/15 g) finely chopped
fresh flat-leaf (Italian) parsley

1 tablespoon extra virgin olive oil

2 teaspoons sherry vinegar or wine vinegar

1 tablespoon salt

1 tablespoon chopped garlic

2 teaspoons dried oregano

1 teaspoon sugar

1 teaspoon ground black pepper

❖ Coarsely chop the tomatoes. Position a food mill fitted with the medium disk over a large bowl and pass the tomatoes through it. (If you do not have a food mill, see recipe hint, right.) Add the cucumber, celery, bell pepper, carrot, onion, parsley, olive oil, vinegar, salt, garlic, oregano, sugar, and pepper and stir well. Transfer to a nonaluminum container, cover, and refrigerate overnight.

❖ Pass the tomato mixture through a food mill fitted with the fine disk. Taste and adjust the seasoning, if necessary. Return the tomato mixture to the container, cover, and refrigerate until well chilled.

❖ Spoon the chilled gazpacho into chilled serving bowls and serve immediately.

recipe hint

If you do not have a food mill, simply chop the tomatoes (step 1) as finely as possible. Do not use a food processor, however, or the bright-red color necessary for the finished soup will be lost. For step 2, simply press the tomato mixture through a fine-mesh sieve using the back of a large spoon.

chilled zucchini soup

serves 4

4 cloves garlic

12 large fresh basil leaves

3 tablespoons extra virgin
olive oil

salt

4 cups (32 fl oz/1 liter) water

13 oz (410 g) ripe tomatoes,
peeled, seeded, and
coarsely chopped

1¼ lb (625 g) zucchini
(courgettes), coarsely grated

2 tablespoons fresh basil
leaves, finely chopped or
shredded, extra

❖ Combine the garlic, large basil leaves, 1 tablespoon of the oil, and salt to taste in a stockpot. Add the water and tomatoes. Stir well and bring to a boil.

❖ Add the zucchini to the stockpot, cover, and cook over low heat for 40 minutes.

❖ Allow the soup to cool a little, then blend or process until smooth. Set aside to cool completely. Cover and refrigerate until chilled.

❖ Serve the chilled soup drizzled with the remaining olive oil and sprinkled with the extra basil.

cucumber
and dill soup

serves 6

3 cucumbers, peeled, seeded,
and chopped

1 onion, chopped

3 tablespoons chopped
fresh dill

3 cups (24 fl oz/750 ml)
chicken stock

½ cup (4 fl oz/125 ml)
heavy (double) cream

❖ Place the cucumbers, onion, 2 tablespoons of the dill, and the stock in a saucepan and bring to a boil over medium heat. Reduce the heat and simmer until the onion is soft.

❖ Allow the soup to cool a little, then purée in a food processor or blender. Return to the pan and stir in the cream.

❖ The soup may be served hot or chilled. If serving hot, reheat slowly; do not allow the soup to boil. If serving chilled, refrigerate, covered, for several hours or until thoroughly chilled. Serve garnished with the remaining dill.

seafood gazpacho

serves 8

4 tomatoes, peeled and seeded

1 medium cucumber, peeled and seeded

1 small red bell pepper (capsicum)

1 yellow pimiento (sweet pepper)

1 medium red (Spanish) onion

2 cloves garlic, finely chopped

dash of Tabasco sauce

1 teaspoon ground cumin

juice of 1 lime

4 cups (32 fl oz/1 liter) tomato juice

2 tablespoons balsamic vinegar

½ cup (4 fl oz/125 ml) olive oil

salt and ground black pepper

¼ cup (⅓ oz/10 g) chopped cilantro (fresh coriander)

1 avocado, finely chopped

1 cup (8 oz/250 g) combined chopped cooked shrimp (prawns) and crab meat

cilantro (fresh coriander) leaves, extra

✤ Finely chop the tomatoes, cucumber, bell pepper, pimiento, and onion and place in a large bowl. Add the garlic, Tabasco, cumin, and lime juice. Add the tomato juice and balsamic vinegar and stir to combine. Stir in the oil. Season with salt and pepper, add the cilantro, and refrigerate until the soup is well chilled.

✤ Just before serving, stir in the avocado and combined shrimp and crab meat. Sprinkle with the extra cilantro and serve.

recipe variations

Try replacing the shrimp and crab meat with small pieces of freshly cooked fish, chopped cooked lobster or even chopped cooked octopus or squid. Or, simply use only shrimp or only crab meat.

chilled
tomato soup
with garlic croutons

serves 4

This soup is a peasant version of gazpacho, the chilled, uncooked Spanish soup that is made using cucumber, tomatoes, onion, bell peppers, bread, olive oil, and garlic.

2 slices day-old, coarse country bread, crusts removed

1 small onion, chopped

2 cloves garlic, finely chopped

1 small cucumber, peeled, seeded, and coarsely chopped

2 lb (1 kg) ripe tomatoes, peeled, seeded, and coarsely chopped

2 small green bell peppers (capsicums), seeded; 1 coarsely chopped, the other finely chopped

½ cup (4 fl oz/125 ml) virgin olive oil

¼ cup (2 fl oz/60 ml) red wine vinegar

salt and ground black pepper

iced water or part iced water and part chilled tomato juice, if needed

Place the bread slices in a bowl, add enough water to cover, and set aside until soft, 3–5 minutes. Remove the bread and squeeze out the excess liquid.

Place the soaked bread, onion, garlic, cucumber, most of the tomatoes, and the coarsely chopped bell pepper in a blender or food processor. Blend or process until the mixture is the desired consistency (it may be chunky or smooth, according to your preference). Transfer to a bowl.

Finely chop the remaining coarsely chopped tomatoes. Add to the bowl along with the finely chopped bell pepper and stir well. Stir in the olive oil, vinegar, and salt and pepper, to taste. If the soup is too thick, add a little of the iced water or mixture of iced water and tomato juice. Cover and refrigerate until well chilled, or for up to 3 days.

Ladle the soup into chilled bowls, top with the garlic croutons (see recipe, right), and serve.

garlic croutons

2 slices coarse country bread

¼ cup (2 fl oz/60 ml) olive oil

1 teaspoon chopped garlic

Cut the bread into ½-inch (13-mm) cubes.

Heat the olive oil in a large saucepan over medium-high heat. Add the garlic and cook, stirring, for 1 minute.

Add the bread cubes and cook, stirring, until golden brown, 4–5 minutes.

Using a slotted spoon, transfer the croutons to paper towels to drain. Serve hot, or allow to cool then store in an airtight container for up to 2 days. Before serving, place on a baking sheet in a moderate oven for 10 minutes to warm and recrisp, if desired.

green gazpacho

serves 4–6

2 slices day-old white bread, crusts removed

1 celery stalk with leaves, chopped

6 tomatillos, husks removed, chopped

1 small green bell pepper (capsicum),
seeded and chopped

2 large or 6 small pickling cucumbers,
peeled and chopped

1 fresh jalapeño chile, stemmed,
seeded (if desired), and chopped

3 cloves garlic, chopped

1 teaspoon salt

juice of 1 lime

1/4 cup (1/3 oz/10 g) coarsely chopped
cilantro (fresh coriander)

2 cups (16 fl oz/500 ml)
vegetable stock or water

MAYONNAISE

2 egg yolks

2 tablespoons tarragon vinegar

1 1/2 teaspoons salt

1/2 teaspoon ground black pepper

2/3 cup (5 fl oz/160 ml) olive oil

chopped fresh chives

1/2 small avocado, stone removed,
flesh peeled and sliced

✤ Place the bread slices in a bowl, add enough water to cover, and set aside until soft, 3–5 minutes. Remove the bread and squeeze out the excess liquid.

✤ Place the celery, tomatillos, bell pepper, cucumbers, jalapeño chile, soaked bread, garlic, salt, lime juice, and cilantro in a food processor. Process until finely puréed. Working in batches, transfer to a blender with the vegetable stock or water and blend until smooth. Set aside.

✤ For the mayonnaise, whisk together the egg yolks, vinegar, salt, and pepper in a large bowl. Gradually add the olive oil, drop by drop, whisking constantly until an emulsion forms. As the mixture thickens, you can begin adding the oil more quickly. (If the mayonnaise becomes too thick or looks stringy, add 1 tablespoon water and then continue.)

✤ When all the oil has been added and the mayonnaise is thick, begin adding the vegetable mixture. Add ¼ cup (2 fl oz/60 ml) at a time, whisking until each addition is thoroughly blended before adding more. Taste and adjust the seasonings. Cover and refrigerate for at least 2 hours or up to 24 hours.

✤ To serve, ladle the soup into chilled bowls. Sprinkle with chopped chives and top each serving with a slice of avocado.

glossary

artichokes

The artichoke is the edible bud of a tall, thistle-like plant. Only the fleshy base of the leaves and the meaty bottom of the bud are eaten; the rest of the leaf and the fuzzy interior choke are discarded. Artichokes are sold fresh year-round, in sizes ranging from very small to very large; they are also available frozen, canned, and marinated. Select compact, heavy globes with tightly closed leaves. Store in a plastic bag in the refrigerator for up to 4 days.

asparagus

This tender stalk with a tightly closed bud is prized for its delicate flavor and subtle hue (white asparagus, a delicacy, is not commonly available). Crisp, straight, firm stalks with a tight cap are best. Wrap in damp paper towels and store in a plastic bag in the refrigerator for up to 4 days.

avocado

This oval-shaped fruit has smooth, buttery flesh with a slightly nutty flavor. To test if an avocado is ripe, lightly press the flesh; it should yield slightly. Store avocados away from heat and light.

basil

With its affinity for sauces and tomato-based dishes, it isn't surprising to find basil in many soup recipes. Intensely aromatic, fresh basil arrives in summer, when tomatoes are at their peak; dried basil may be found on the spice shelf year-round. Store freshly cut stems in a glass with a little water, covered with plastic wrap, in the refrigerator for up to 2 days.

bell peppers

Also known as capsicums, these colorful, crunchy vegetable–fruits are related to chiles, although they are far milder in taste. They change color as they ripen, from green to orange, yellow, red, or purple. They can be eaten raw, added to salads, or cooked, when they become much sweeter and softer. Store in a plastic bag in the refrigerator for up to 1 week.

broccoli

Both the rigid green stalks and the tightly packed dark-green or purplish-green heads (also called florets) are edible. Choose firm stalks and closed heads with deep color and no yellow areas. Store in a plastic bag in the refrigerator for up to 4 days.

carrots

Choose firm, bright-orange carrots; avoid those that are droopy or have cracks or dry spots. Store them in a plastic bag, tops removed, in the refrigerator for up to 2 weeks. Either peel or scrub carrots before using. Tiny baby carrots are actually a separate variety, prized for their delicate flavor and charming appearance. Store them as you would regular carrots.

chickpeas

Also known as garbanzo beans, chickpeas are medium-sized, light-brown, wrinkled peas with a nutty flavor. Available dried or canned, they are used in many Middle Eastern, Mediterranean, and Indian dishes.

chives

The long, hollow green leaves of this herb add bright color and a mild onion flavor to many dishes when snipped into little pieces. Fresh chives should not be wilted or damaged. Wrap in damp paper towels and store in a plastic bag in the refrigerator for up to 4 days.

cilantro

Also known as fresh coriander, this strongly flavored herb is very popular in Asian, Indian, Latin American, and Middle Eastern cooking. To store, rinse under cold running water and shake dry, then wrap in paper towels and keep in a plastic bag in the refrigerator for up to 1 week.

fava beans

Also known as broad beans, these are large, slightly flattened, green or light-brown beans. When they are very young, the whole pod can be eaten, but usually they are shelled like peas. Fava beans are available fresh, frozen, and dried.

fennel

With its tubular stalks and feathery leaves, this bulbous, creamy-white to pale-green vegetable resembles celery, but its flavor hints of licorice. Fresh fennel is delicious raw or cooked; dried fennel seeds are used as a seasoning. Select bulbs that are free of cracks or brown spots. Store in a plastic bag in the refrigerator for up to 4 days.

garlic

A bulb with a papery outer skin, a head of garlic is composed of numerous small cloves. Garlic may be used as a savory seasoning for every savory course of a meal. It is aromatic and almost bitter when raw, but becomes delicate and sweet when cooked. Fresh garlic should be plump and firm. Store whole garlic bulbs in a cool, dark, dry place.

ginger

The rhizome, or underground stem, of a semitropical plant, fresh ginger is a pungent seasoning with a lively, hot flavor and peppery aroma. Select stems that are firm and heavy, never shrivelled, with taut, glossy skin. Wrap in a paper towel and store in the refrigerator for up to 2 days. For longer storage, wrap airtight and freeze the unpeeled root.

kale

A member of the cabbage family, kale has ruffled dark-green leaves and tastes similar to its cabbage relatives. It is eaten fresh or cooked, or can be used as a decorative garnish. Wash the leaves, dry well, and then store in a paper towel-lined plastic bag in the refrigerator for up to 3 days.

leeks

Although closely related to the onion, this long, white, tubular bulb with broad, flattish leaves has a much milder flavor. Cut off the roots, trim the tops, and wash well before using. Store in a plastic bag in the refrigerator for up to 1 week.

lentils

Lentils come in several shapes and colors, but the most common are green (or brown) lentils when whole. Red lentils are slightly smaller, and they fade to yellow when they are cooked. Lentils are sold dried, either whole, split, or ground into flour. Wash lentils well under cold running water before using them.

olive oil

A staple of Mediterranean cooking, olive oil imparts a clean, fruity flavor and golden-to-green color to salad dressings, grilled bread, and pasta sauces. Use extra-virgin oils, from the first pressing, for cold dishes. For sauces, use milder oils that can stand up to heat. Store in a dark spot away from heat for 6 months, or in the refrigerator for a year. (Chilled oil may become thick and cloudy; let it warm to room temperature before using.)

oregano

Aromatic and robustly flavored, oregano is a favorite herb of Italian and Greek cooks. Select bright-green fresh oregano with firm stems. it is also available dried, both whole and ground, in the spice section of the supermarket. Refrigerate fresh oregano in a plastic bag for up to 3 days.

parsley

Widely used for cooking and as a garnish, parsley has such a clean, refreshing flavor that it is sometimes enjoyed as an after-meal digestive. Curly-leaf parsley is mild, while flat-leaf (Italian) parsley is more pungent. Select healthy, lively looking bunches. To store, rinse under cold running water and shake dry, then wrap in paper towels and keep in a plastic bag in the refrigerator for up to 1 week.

pumpkin

Also known as "winter squash," pumpkins have a very hard rind covering a firm, sweetish yellow or orange flesh. They range in size from very small to very large, depending on the variety. Pumpkins are usually peeled and cut into sections before cooking. Store whole pumpkins in a cool, dry place for 2–3 months. Once cut, remove the seeds, wrap well in plastic wrap, and store in the refrigerator for up to 3 days.

squash

Slender, soft-skinned green and yellow zucchini, straight and crookneck squashes, and pattypan squashes are classified as "summer" vegetables, although many are sold year-round. Select heavy, well-shaped squash without cracks or bruises. Store for up to 4 days in the refrigerator.

tomatoes

Although they are botanically a fruit, tomatoes are eaten as a vegetable. Oval-shaped plum tomatoes (also called Italian or Roma) are thick and meaty, with less juice and smaller seeds than other varieties, which makes them ideal for soups and stews. They are sold fresh, or in cans sometimes flavored with basil and other seasonings. Other market forms include stewed tomatoes, cooked with celery, onions, and seasonings; tomato paste, a highly concentrated purée; and sweet, chewy sun-dried tomatoes, either plain or packed in oil.

index

Page numbers in italics refer to photographs.

a note on measurements

U.S. cup measurements are used throughout this book. Slight adjustments may need to be made to quantities if Imperial or metric measures are used.

acknowledgments

Weldon Owen wishes to thank the following people for their assistance in the production of this book: Angela Handley (editorial assistance); Nancy Sibtain (indexing).

vegetable ga
broth steam
vichyssoise c
seafood stoc
muffins boui
chicken cons